THE BIRTHRIGHT
AND
THE BLESSING
Pleasing God With Your Personal Finances

THE BIRTHRIGHT
AND
THE BLESSING
Pleasing God With Your Personal Finances

DR. MARK BOSJE

Copyright © 2014
Dr. Mark Bosje
First Printing – July 2014

ISBN 10: 1490473157
ISBN 13: 978-1490473154

All Scripture quotations are from the King James Version

All rights reserved.
Before printing any portion of this book,
please contact the author for written permission.
e-mail:mbosje@yahoo.com

Acknowledgements

Just like handling finances, writing a book is a team effort. Although the truths in this book come straight from the Bible, they could never have been presented in this format without a tremendous amount of help from a great group of people. I offer you all my sincere thanks.

My dad got me started in finances at the age of twelve. He bought my first accounting ledger, helped me to get my first job, and taught me how to tithe. My mom taught me to love the Bible. My parents have been pillars of support my entire life. Mom and Dad, I thank you both with all of my heart.

My nephew, Tim Reed, first encouraged me to write a book on finances. Bob Marshall and Linda Stubblefield gave me advice on the formatting and the design for this book. John Cole created the cover design. Alex Midence took the cover photo. Shari House volunteered many hours of proofreading and provided some very insightful comments. Thank you to each one of you.

Wayne Sheaffer has been an amazing example of integrity and my inspiration for chapter five. My brother-in-law, Chris Senecal, and my fellow laborer, Scott Mercer, are excellent examples of active investors. Chad Inman and I regularly share passive investment ideas. I thank each one of you for being a true friend.

My dear wife has supported me every step of the way. This is as much her book as mine. Thank you, Sweetheart. Our seven children have been very patient with me throughout this project. Thank you Matthew, Sarah, Rebekah, Anna, Nathan, Elizabeth, and Alyssa. You are the best family in the world. I love you all so much.

Most of all, I would like to thank my amazing God. Not only has He saved me from all my sin and promised me an eternal home in Heaven, but He has also provided me with the perfect manual by which to live my life until I get there.

Table of Contents

INTRODUCTION	1
WHAT IS A STEWARD?	5
A FAITHFUL STEWARD	13
GOD'S THREE TESTS	21
MONEY IS NOT EVIL	29
THE KEY INGREDIENT	37
ONLY THE BY-PRODUCT	43
YOUR FINANCIAL STATE	51
A BUDGET THAT WORKS	57
WHAT IS THE TITHE?	67
DEALING WITH DEBT	73
ELIMINATING DEBT	83
SAVING FOR WINTER	89
WISE INVESTING	93
LAYING UP TREASURES	101
THE VERY BEST THING	105
A LONG TERM GOAL	111
MONEY THAT WORKS	117
THE NEXT GENERATION	123
DEFINING SUCCESS	127
159 VERSES FROM PROVERBS	131
FINANCIAL WORKSHEETS	145
Worksheet 1 – Income	147
Worksheet 2 – Bills	148
Worksheet 3 – Debts	149
Worksheet 4 – Possessions	150
Worksheet 5 – Assets	151
Worksheet 6 – Cash Flow Statement	152
Worksheet 7 – Balance Sheet	153

Introduction

The idea for this book began many years ago in the beautiful country of New Zealand. My wife and I had been missionaries for five years in the city of Wanganui on the North Island. Beginning with the two of us and our three young children, we had planted a new church. God's hand of blessing on the work was obvious.

Our church was averaging over 150 people in the Sunday morning services. We welcomed first-time visitors every week, and people were regularly being saved and baptized. We had just purchased and renovated a building in the center of the city, and the weekly offerings were easily covering the budget.

We had a significant presence in our area, we were hosting two national conferences each year, and we in turn were supporting a large number of foreign missionaries. In the eyes of many people I was a success.

In one area of my life, however, I knew that I was a failure. For some time I had wanted to teach a series of Bible studies on the subject of finances, but when I began studying for the initial lessons I felt overwhelmed. My own personal finances were a disaster. I was nearly $20,000 in debt to credit card companies. I had next to nothing put aside in savings.

Even worse, I had used an exemption available to ministers of religion and opted out of Social Security. I had made a declaration to the United States government that I believed it was my personal responsibility to care for my own future and the future of my family, but since that time I had done nothing in order to prepare.

It quickly became clear to me that two things needed to happen before I could teach my church members God's plan for their finances: I had to understand His plan, and I had to begin following it. I began months of intense Bible study on the subject of money. This book you are now reading is the result of that study.

From the beginning I attempted to study the subject without a preconceived opinion. I had no desire to twist the Bible to fit what I already thought was true. As much as was humanly possible, I went to the Word of God with an open mind to learn what He had to say on the subject.

I began my studies in the book of Proverbs. King Solomon was inspired by the Holy Spirit to write Proverbs. He was both wealthy and wise. When Solomon addressed the subject of money he knew what he was talking about. I found that there are 159 verses in the book of Proverbs which refer directly to the subject of money. These verses are listed in an appendix in the back of this book. Many other verses in Proverbs contain principles that can be applied to the subject of money.

After finishing with the book of Proverbs, I began to study every other verse I could find in the Bible that referred to money. There are literally thousands. In fact, money is one of the most mentioned subjects in the Word of God. Although some Christians may be hesitant to discuss money, God is definitely not!

I began to group together verses which addressed similar subjects, and then to arrange them into a simple plan. As the pieces of the puzzle fell into place, one thing became very clear. The Bible gives us a definite plan for our money.

I was raised in a Christian home by Godly parents. I am extremely blessed in this respect. The principles that my father and mother taught me as a child have been confirmed as I studied the Scriptures.

I have also read hundreds of books on the subject of finances. I have listened to countless sermons, attended numerous seminars, and counselled with other pastors about money. Each principle that I have learned has been carefully examined in the light of the Word of God before being implemented. It is my desire to please the Lord in this area of my life as in all others.

Introduction

It is also my desire to be a help to other Christians who find their finances to be a burden. This book is not a plan to help you get rich. This book is a plan to help you please God with your money.

I have now been pastoring for more than seventeen years. Without doubt, the area where people have most often asked for my help is in the area of finances. Many good Christians are severely limited in their ability to serve the Lord because they are financially incapable of doing so. Many good churches are in financial trouble because their members are in financial trouble. This should not be the case.

No two people are at the same stage in their financial life. Everyone's situation is different, but the same Biblical principles apply to everyone. Our problems are never caused by the principles that God has given us in His Word. Our problems are always caused by ignorance of those principles or by a lack of application.

If you are discouraged, let me assure you that there is hope. God's Word never fails us. I have never counseled anyone who was unable to get out of financial trouble if they just did what God told them to do. There really is a light at the end of the tunnel.

I hope that you are able to enjoy reading these written words as if you were listening to a friend.

What Is a Steward?

The title and position of steward is well-established both in the Word of God and throughout history. The steward was a representative of his master whose responsibilities varied according to his ability.[1] His duties ranged from caring for the domestic routine of the household to representing his lord as an ambassador in a foreign country.

We know that Abram had a steward named Eliezer of Damascus. Prior to the birth of Ishmael and Isaac, Abram had elevated Eliezer to a position equal to that of being his son and his heir.[2] Stewards in Bible times were often treated like members of the family.

After Joseph was promoted to the second highest position in the land of Egypt, he also had a steward. This steward had the authority to speak on his master's behalf, to release a prisoner from his cell, and to provide for the needs of any guests.[3] Joseph's steward also had the right to distribute his master's money.[4]

It was the custom of kings in the Bible to have a steward and occasionally many stewards. King Elah had a steward named Arza.[5] King Herod's steward was named Chuza.[6] King David had numerous stewards who oversaw his substance and his possessions.[7]

In one of the parables Jesus taught, the lord of the vineyard had a steward who paid his master's employees.[8] Jesus also taught that the wise and faithful steward is the one who provides for those whom the lord has placed under his authority.[9] Jesus even taught one entire parable about an unjust steward, comparing him to the children of this world who in their generation are wiser than the children of light.[10]

The Apostle Paul gave the bishop special recognition as the steward of God.[11] This title has the implication of being the superintendent, or the business manager, of the church. This reference is of specific importance to every pastor.

Every child of God has been given the responsibility of stewardship.[12] We have been elevated to the position of a son.[13] We have been given the command and the authority to speak on behalf of our Lord.[14] We are empowered to free captives from prison.[15] We have been ordered to provide for the needs of others. We are commanded to care for our own households as well as for the household of God.[16] We represent Him as His ambassadors to this world.[17]

As a Christian there is no question of whether or not you are a steward of God. Nothing that you have is really yours. You did not bring anything into this world, and you are not taking anything out.[18] Your house, your vehicle, your money, your children, and even your life – everything has been loaned to you for a short time.[19] The question you should be asking yourself is, "What kind of steward am I?"

You do not have the right to manage your Master's money and goods according to your own desires. It is every steward's responsibility to determine his Lord's wishes and to govern his decisions accordingly. You are a servant of your Lord, and your life belongs to Him. You must handle all of your money realizing that all of it is His money. As the Lord gives you more money, you must continue to make your decisions for handling that money based on what your Master wants and not on your own wants and wishes.

If you desire to be a good Christian, then you must be a good steward. If you want to be a good steward, then you must learn how to handle your money according to God's principles.

This introduces a whole new concept. We all have to learn about money! For many Christians the subject of money is a painful one. It has been a burden for most of their lives, and when they think about how little money they have and how much money they owe, they feel like a failure. Since most people do not enjoy talking about something at which they feel like a failure, they will often avoid the subject completely.

Some people feel as though they should already know everything about money. They use it every day. They earn money, they spend money, they borrow money, they owe money, and they even have some money in their wallet. To admit that they are ignorant about money would make them feel foolish so they just keep their mouth shut and carry on through life with their finances in shambles.

Some Christians feel that it is not spiritual to discuss money. Although they may not express that thought verbally, whenever the subject of money comes up, they feel like it would be too worldly for them to discuss it. Like politics or sex, money is one of those subjects that we avoid discussing while it takes our country and our children down the road to destruction.

No one can become a good steward without thinking, talking, reading, studying, and learning about money.

Some preachers avoid the subject of money for fear they will be perceived as greedy. These same preachers then complain that there is not enough money to do everything that God wants done. They may teach their people to tithe, but they are fearful to go beyond that point. They leave their sheep to find their own way through this complicated subject.

If we don't *think* about money, if we don't *talk* about money, and if we don't *study* about money, how can we be good stewards? If our children are not learning the laws of money from the Word of God, from where and from whom will they learn them?

A STEWARD IS NOT BORN WITH SOME SECRET KNOWLEDGE

Those in financial difficulties will occasionally look at someone who seems to be succeeding and decide that person must have been born lucky. They may even believe that somewhere there is a secret conspiracy that is keeping them poor. They may feel that other people are on the inside, and that they are somehow stuck on the outside.

Those who handle their money well were not born with a secret money gene that you did not get. They do not have special DNA. They were not born lucky. Anyone can learn God's plan for their money if they will make the effort.[20]

A STEWARD MUST LEARN THE LAWS OF MONEY

"Yea, if thou criest after knowledge, and liftest up thy voice for understanding; If thou seekest her as silver, and searchest for her as for hid treasures; Then shalt thou understand the fear of the LORD, and find the knowledge of God." Proverbs 2:3-5

Did you notice that we are commanded to lift up our voices for understanding? We are supposed to ask questions, and we are supposed to learn. This means that we should be trying to find the answers about money as much as we are trying to find the money.

Instead of spending so much time with sports, hobbies, surfing the internet, watching television, or shopping, God expects His children to pick up His Book and learn about handling His money so that they will know what to do with it when He gives it to them.

God is not poor. He is always looking for good stewards.[21]

God is *never* lacking in money. He is lacking people who know what to do with money. When you prove to Him that you have learned how to be a good steward, God will eventually take money away from those who have not learned His principles and give it to you.[22]

IF A STEWARD GETS MONEY WITHOUT LEARNING THE LAWS, HE WILL LOSE THE MONEY

"An inheritance may be gotten hastily at the beginning; but the end thereof shall not be blessed." Proverbs 20:21

Many people think that the answer to their financial dilemma is to get a raise, to receive an inheritance, or maybe to win the lottery.

The facts show that if you are in financial trouble and suddenly receive a large sum of money, you will be right back in trouble in a very short time. Getting money without knowing God's principles may even get you in greater trouble than you were before.

You may think a million dollars would solve all your problems. If you are in financial trouble, it is not because you don't have enough money. It is because you do not know the principles for handling the money you already have.

A STEWARD MUST LEARN THE LAWS OF MONEY FROM SOMEONE WHO KNOWS THEM

"He that walketh with wise men shall be wise: but a companion of fools shall be destroyed." Proverbs 13:20

One of the hallmarks of our society today is that we easily pay attention to those who have failed in the area they teach. People seek advice on marriage from divorcees. They are willing to learn about raising children from people who have none of their own.

People will accept opinions on morality from homosexuals, take anger management classes from people with terrible tempers, go to rehabilitation to learn from alcoholics, and accept financial advice from people that are broke. Taking advice from those who do not, or cannot, practice what they preach is a dangerous practice.

You should never take advice from someone on the subject of money unless you know that they have learned God's principles for money. The Bible teaches us to get our wisdom from the wise.[23]

The financial principles that you will learn in this book are not theories. They are being used by many people that are financially fit today. They are being used by pastors and missionaries and Christian businesspeople and housewives and teenagers all over the world who have decided that God is the highest authority on how they should handle their money.

A STEWARD MUST APPLY THE RULES

"A wise man will hear, and will increase learning; and a man of understanding shall attain unto wise counsels:" Proverbs 1:5

No matter where you are in your financial life, you can immediately begin to use these Biblical principles. As you read through this book, ask God to show you what to do now. Do not make excuses. Just start where you are. You can never begin yesterday, and tomorrow is too late. Today is always the right day to begin!

Ignorance is no longer an excuse. Not being good with money is no longer a reason to fail. You have a responsibility to learn and apply the laws that your Master has given you to govern His money.

All of the verses quoted in this chapter are found in the book of Proverbs. The Bible tells us that Solomon was the wisest man alive.[24] God inspired Solomon to write a book about wisdom.

The book of Proverbs has 915 verses, and 159 of those verses teach specifically on the subject of money. That is more than one out of every six verses! Many more verses in Proverbs refer indirectly to money. So according to the wisest man on earth, at least one-sixth of wisdom relates directly to how you handle your finances.

STEWARDS MUST TEACH THE RULES TO THEIR CHILDREN

"Train up a child in the way he should go: and when he is old, he will not depart from it." Proverbs 22:6

Some parents never talk about money with their children. Maybe they don't want their children to know how much they themselves are struggling. Maybe they do not have any idea what to teach their children. Maybe they feel that their children should somehow find out on their own. Since these children are raised to be uncomfortable talking about money, they will one day be unable to discuss it with their children.

As you begin to apply these principles, talk them over with your friends and family. Teach your children to apply these principles to their one dollar the same way that you apply them to your one hundred dollars. Your children may be taught to add and subtract in school, but they are rarely taught to be financially responsible. In our country this area is still left entirely up to the parents.

Jesus preached many times on the subject of money. Paul spoke on the area of finances in a number of passages. The Word of God has a multitude of examples and illustrations from which we can learn how to care for our own money. The subject of money is just as spiritual as any other subject in the Bible.

[1] Matthew 25:15
[2] Genesis 15:1-3
[3] Genesis 43:18-24
[4] Genesis 44:1
[5] 1 Kings 16:9
[6] Luke 8:3
[7] 1 Chronicles 28:1
[8] Matthew 20:8
[9] Luke 12:42
[10] Luke 16:1-9
[11] Titus 1:7
[12] 1 John 3:17
[13] John 1:12
[14] Acts 1:8
[15] Isaiah 61:1; Luke 4:18
[16] 1 Timothy 5:8; Luke 12:42; Galatians 6:10
[17] 2 Corinthians 5:20
[18] Job 1:21; 1 Timothy 6:7
[19] 1 Corinthians 6:19
[20] 2 Timothy 2:15
[21] 2 Chronicles 16:9
[22] Matthew 25:29; Luke 19:26
[23] Proverbs 22:17
[24] 1 Kings 4:30, 31

A Faithful Steward

Some Christians seem to have picked up the idea that none of us should have much money. In some churches there appears to be an unspoken law that if you are spiritual, then you must be poor – or at least struggling!

Those Christians who do have money are made to feel slightly ashamed for their prosperity, and the greedy rich are blamed for everyone else's woes. After all, if those wealth mongers would just stop taking all the money from the poor then there would be that much more to go around. Obviously, they are backslidden!

These same critics and naysayers are constantly hindered from serving the Lord because of a lack of finances. Buildings are not built, equipment is not purchased, missionaries are not sent, and communities are not reached because there is not enough money to get the job done.

Have you ever noticed that those that do the most for the Lord's work are those that have the money to do it? They quietly give, support missionaries, and help the poor because they can!

Dear reader, you need to understand that being rich, being poor, or being anywhere in between has absolutely nothing to do with your level of spirituality. Please read these four lines out loud very slowly and carefully:

> **You can be ungodly and poor.**
> **You can be ungodly and rich.**
> **You can be spiritual and poor.**
> **You can be spiritual and rich.**

We are going to look at some Bible examples of all four of these situations. You will see that money is not proof of anything when it comes to your spirituality. The only way to know if you are right with God in any area is if you are obedient to Him in that area.

Our job is to obey. It is God's prerogative to give the results that please Him. It is a big mistake to decide whether anyone is the sort of Christian that they ought to be depending on the level of their personal finances.

YOU CAN BE UNGODLY AND POOR

Millions of people around this world are starving in abject poverty and have never heard the name of Jesus Christ. Muslims, Buddhists, Hindus, and atheists are often poor, but it is certainly not because they are right with God. They are ungodly, and they are poor.

Jeremiah said of the idolatrous Jews who were left behind during the captivity, *"Surely these are poor; they are foolish: for they know not the way of the LORD, nor the judgment of their God."* [1] Here is a Biblical example of a group of people that were not following God, and they were poor.

YOU CAN BE UNGODLY AND RICH

In the book of Luke, Jesus tells a story of a certain rich man.[2] Whenever Jesus told a story of a *"certain man,"* you can be *"certain"* that he was a real *"man."* In Jesus' story this fellow was doing well financially. His farm had produced so much grain that he was planning to tear down his old barns and build some great big shiny new barns. God called this man a fool. He was not a fool because he had done well on his farm, but because he was *"not rich toward God."*

We find another example in the story of Ananias and Sapphira.[3] They were rich enough to sell their property and give some of the money away, but the Holy Spirit killed them because of a severe heart problem.

These are Biblical examples of people that were rich, but they were not right with God. You may have noticed that neither story ended well. They died because of their sin, not because of their money.

YOU CAN BE SPIRITUAL AND POOR

This next statement may be a slap in the face to the "health and wealth" type evangelists that equate riches with spiritual success. Spiritual people can be broke! Your finances are not connected to your spirituality. It is very dangerous to assume that once you get enough money, you will be spiritually acceptable to God.

There were times Jesus was poor. When a potential disciple wanted to follow Him, Jesus responded, *"Foxes have holes, and birds of the air have nests; but the Son of man hath not where to lay his head."* [4]

The Apostle Paul told the Philippians, *"I know both how to be abased, and I know how to abound: everywhere and in all things I am instructed both to be full and to be hungry, both to abound and to suffer need."* [5] Paul's spirituality did not rise and fall based on the number of coins he had in his pocket.

YOU CAN BE SPIRITUAL AND RICH

You may feel like anyone who is wealthy must have done something dishonest to get it. Since the Bible says you cannot serve God and mammon, can we assume these rich people must have turned their back on God at some point in order to get all that money? I realize this is the way that some good people think. Allow me to surprise you as we look at some of the spiritual heroes in the Word of God.

Let's begin with Job in the Old Testament. The Bible describes Job as perfect, upright, one that feared God, and one that eschewed — or ran away from — evil.[6] Wow! What a complimentary description.

The Bible also tells us that Job had ten children, and then immediately begins to catalogue his tremendous wealth.[7] First of all, Job owned 7,000 sheep. The price for one sheep can vary greatly, but in today's money one full-grown sheep is worth approximately $50. That means anyone owning 7,000 sheep today would have $350,000 worth of sheep.

Keep in mind that at this time in Bible history a man's wealth was measured by the size of his flocks and herds. All of these sheep would be the equivalent of Job's savings account.

Next, we learn that Job owned 3,000 camels. Camels are a little more difficult to put a price on since they are not commonly sold here in our country. Camels were the main means of transportation and perhaps comparable to a car today. Do you know anyone that owns 3,000 cars? Maybe Job had a used camel business.

Next, the Bible tells us that Job owned 500 yoke of oxen. A yoke was a pair of oxen trained to work together. They were used exactly the same way that farmers use tractors today. I don't know how much money 500 tractors would be worth in today's market, but I do know that it would be a lot! I personally don't know any farmers rich enough to have that many tractors. Consider that even if these 1,000 animals were sold for meat, one full grown ox equals about $3,000 worth of beef at the butcher shop. That is $3,000,000 just for the meat!

Then, we find that Job had 500 she asses. Donkeys were the beasts of burdens, comparable to a pickup truck or a trailer. Female donkeys also have the potential to produce more donkeys.

Lastly, we learn that Job had a very great household. He had a lot of tents, furniture, dishes, clothes, servants, and all the other things that we equate with wealth. He was super rich; a multi-millionaire. He was in the Forbes 500 of the Bible. No one else around was as well-off as Job. He was spiritual, and he was rich.

When God gave the devil permission to put Job to the test, Job lost everything that he had. This was not a result of any sin or failure on Job's part. God looked at this trial as a compliment.

Job's response to his impoverishment was, *"Naked came I out of my mother's womb, and naked shall I return thither: the LORD gave, and the LORD hath taken away; blessed be the name of the LORD."*[8]

Job went from being spiritual and rich to being spiritual and poor. He then said, *"Though he slay me, yet will I trust in him: but I will maintain mine own ways before him."*[9]

In the last chapter of the book, God told Job's three friends that they were going to be in big trouble unless they offered a sacrifice. Job then prayed for them. After that, we find that Job got back everything he had before his trials, only doubled.[10] Job even had twice as many children – ten on earth and ten in Heaven.

So Job went from being *spiritual and rich* to being *spiritual and poor* and then back to being *spiritual and rich* again. Job's financial condition varied greatly, but all through the book he was righteous. If you can be spiritual with money or spiritual without money, wouldn't it be better to have the money? The Bible clearly tells us that we cannot serve God and mammon, but we cannot serve God without mammon either!

MORE WEALTHY PEOPLE IN THE BIBLE

Abraham
Abraham was an entrepreneur. He owned a business that employed 318 people.[11] One entire chapter in the book of Genesis is the record of one of his real estate transactions. His wife Sarah had died, and Abraham bought a field with a cave on one end of it so that he could bury her properly. He paid cash! [12]

Isaac
"And Abraham gave all that he had unto Isaac."[13] *"Then Isaac sowed in that land, and received in the same year an hundredfold:* (That is 10,000% interest in one year!) *and the LORD blessed him. And the man waxed great, and went forward, and grew until he became very great: For he had possession of flocks, and possessions of herds, and great store of servants: and the Philistines envied him."*[14] Isaac inherited his father's wealth and then grew it until he was fantastically rich. Isaac was a man that loved God, and yet he was so wealthy that his unbelieving neighbors envied him.

Jacob

Here we find a man who left home so broke that he had to use stones for his pillow.[15] When Jacob tried to resign his job fourteen years later, his uncle Laban told him that he could name his salary if he would stay.[16] When Jacob finally arrived back home, he tried to give his estranged brother about $100,000 worth of animals.[17]

Joseph

By the time he was thirty years old, Joseph was the head of the Internal Revenue Service for the wealthiest nation on the planet. He had gold, silver, a royal Ferrari (um...chariot), and was the second highest power in the land.[18] He was also rich enough to bring his entire extended family of seventy people down to Egypt, to buy them property, and then to support them.[19]

Pharaoh put Joseph in this position because Pharaoh could see that the Spirit of God was in him. Joseph was obviously rich and spiritual at the same time.

Boaz

Boaz was another businessman who was an ancestor of Jesus Christ. He owned large tracts of real estate and hired a group of young men to work for him. Boaz had enough workers that he had to hire at least one supervisor.[20]

When Boaz decided to marry Ruth he bought the entire belongings of three men in one day.[21] He was also able to take very good care of his mother-in-law.

David

God took David from watching his father's sheep in the back fields to being the wealthiest man in Israel. Throughout the forty and a half years of his reign, David became incredibly rich. The gold in just one of David's crowns was worth $40,000, and that is not counting all of the inlaid precious jewels.[22] It would take a whole chapter in this book just to catalogue David's wealth. David was also named as a man after God's own heart.[23]

Solomon

When God asked Solomon what he wanted and Solomon asked for wisdom, God was so pleased that He promised to make him rich as well as wise.[24] Solomon's wealth was beyond calculation.

Everything Solomon built, both for his own house and for God's temple, was made of gold. The furniture, the décor, and even the walls were covered with gold. It has been estimated that it cost the equivalent of $10,000,000,000 (ten billion dollars!) to build that temple.[25] Solomon had so much money in his kingdom that silver was treated like stones on the side of the road.[26]

Barnabas

This New Testament investor saw that his church had some needs. He put a "For Sale" sign on one of his properties, and when it sold he took the whole amount down to the church and gave it to the pastors.[27] At the same time Barnabas was spiritual enough that his pastor gave him the title "son of consolation," and God called him into His full-time ministry.[28]

Paul

Paul made an interesting statement in Philippians 4:12. He said, *"I know how to abound."* He was saying, "I know how to handle it when things are going well financially." In order to learn this, Paul must have had times when things were good. However, Paul also learned how to handle the lean times. Neither was the *result* of his spirituality. His *response* to each situation showed his spirituality.

I have written this chapter with the assumption that you want to be spiritual, but it is crucial that you see the lack of connection between your finances and the level of your spirituality.

Being successful with your money does not indicate that you have arrived spiritually. Being spiritual does not guarantee that your finances will improve. Your goal should be to live a life that pleases God while handling your finances according to the principles that God has given us and then to leave the results to Him.

If God has given us the task of reaching the world for Christ, and He has also given us the responsibility of being the steward of His finances, then we should desire to succeed in both areas. The ungodly will not serve God whether they have any money or not. The spiritual person who has little or no money may have the right desires but will accomplish little for God without the funds to make it happen. The one who loves God and has the money to move forward for Him will be able to accomplish much for His Kingdom.

[1] Jeremiah 5:4
[2] Luke 12:16-21
[3] Acts 5:1-11
[4] Luke 9:58
[5] Philippians 4:12
[6] Job 1:1
[7] Job 1:2, 3
[8] Job 1:21
[9] Job 13:15
[10] Job 42:12, 13
[11] Genesis 14:14
[12] Genesis 23
[13] Genesis 25:25
[14] Genesis 26:12-14
[15] Genesis 28:11
[16] Genesis 30:28
[17] Genesis 32:14, 15
[18] Genesis 41:38-49
[19] Genesis 47:5, 6
[20] Ruth 2:3-5
[21] Ruth 4:1-9
[22] 2 Samuel 12:30; 1 Chronicles 20:2
[23] Acts 13:22
[24] 1 Kings 3:11-13
[25] 2 Chronicles 3:4-10
[26] 1 Kings 10:27
[27] Acts 4:36, 37
[28] Acts 13:2

GOD'S THREE TESTS

"He that is faithful in that which is least is faithful also in much: and he that is unjust in the least is unjust also in much. If therefore ye have not been faithful in the unrighteous mammon, who will commit to your trust the true riches? And if ye have not been faithful in that which is another man's, who shall give you that which is your own? No servant can serve two masters: for either he will hate the one, and love the other; or else he will hold to the one, and despise the other. Ye cannot serve God and mammon."
Luke 16:10-13

God works by commands and principles. He gives us these commands and principles in His Word, and then He makes it clear that He never changes. You will never find success in any area of your life by trying to slip past or circumvent God's commands and principles for that area. You will never fool Him, and you will never convince Him that you should be the exception.

"For I am the LORD, I change not; therefore ye sons of Jacob are not consumed." Malachi 3:6

"Jesus Christ the same yesterday, and to day, and for ever."
Hebrews 13:8

One of God's principles is that He tests His people before He commits Himself to use them in a greater way. In other words, God gives you a trial run and then, depending on how you respond, He may reward you with more responsibility. People often fail God's tests because they do not even realize they are being tested. This is especially true in the area of money. In Luke 16 Jesus Christ explains three tests that God uses:

THE TEST OF LITTLE THINGS

"He that is faithful in that which is least is faithful also in much: and he that is unjust in the least is unjust also in much." Luke 16:10

God will give someone a small task to test their faithfulness. If He knows they are faithful with something that they perceive as small, God knows they will be faithful when it is something much bigger.

If someone decides that these little things don't really matter, then God knows He cannot trust them with anything more important. If you are wondering why God is not blessing your financial situation, perhaps you could ask yourself a few questions:

- Have you been given a job by your boss, parent, pastor, teacher, or any other authority in which you did less than your best?

- Do you only do your best when someone is watching?

- Have you purchased things which have been quickly destroyed because of a lack of maintenance, neglect, or carelessness?

- Do you get up early?[1]

- Do you make your bed, keep your room clean, polish your shoes, iron your clothes, and have good personal hygiene?

These are the types of things that God watches to determine whether you are faithful enough for Him to trust you with bigger things. If you asked someone to do something that never got done, if you continually caught them slacking off, if you gave them things which were quickly ruined, if they overslept or kept a dirty house or smelled bad, would you give them any more responsibility?

I would not, you would not, and neither does God! God knows that people will do a large task at the same level of character that they do the little things.

THE TEST OF UNRIGHTEOUS MAMMON

"If therefore ye have not been faithful in the unrighteous mammon, who will commit to your trust the true riches?" Luke 16:11

When God speaks of "unrighteous mammon," He is not saying that money is wicked. It is simply mammon that is "not righteous." Although money can be treacherous, it has no morality of its own. The right or wrong of money is decided by what you do with it.

Here we learn that God will give you money, which itself is not right or wrong, to see what you will do with it. If your money is handled correctly, then God knows that He can trust you with more. One of the tests you must pass before getting more money is using the money you already have in the right way.

Many people deceive themselves into thinking that if they had more money things would be different. If they had more money they would tithe. If they had more money they would pay their bills on time. If they had more money they would be kind and generous.

If this is your way of thinking, you are fooling yourself. If you had more money, you would do exactly what you are doing now but on a larger scale. You would tithe, and pay bills, and help people just as much as you are doing right now. If you are not passing this test, getting more money will not change anything. You can try to fool yourself, but you cannot fool God.[2] Before He will give you more money, you must prove that you know what to do with what you have. You have to pass His tests.

The true riches mentioned in this verse include a lot more than just cash. The sad fact is that many Christians do not have victory in their Christian life at least partially because they handle their money unwisely. If you have unsaved loved ones, a Sunday school class that does not grow, a lack of influence with friends and neighbors, or disharmony in your marriage or your home, then perhaps it is time that you examine your personal money habits.

THE TEST OF OTHER PEOPLE'S THINGS

"And if ye have not been faithful in that which is another man's, who shall give you that which is your own?" Luke 16:12

When you choose to borrow something that belongs to someone else, God is watching you. It may be a tool or a cup of sugar or a book that you borrowed from a neighbor or a friend. In fact, if this book is not yours, God is testing you with it!

In Bible days, things were almost always paid for immediately or returned the same day. Today we live by credit. We have grown accustomed to carrying these financial obligations. This is not necessarily wrong, but the obligations do not go away. If you have a mortgage, you borrowed someone else's money to pay for it. A car payment means that some portion of your car is borrowed. Most people pay for their electricity after they have already used it.

The way that you handle your obligations and the way that you pay your bills determine whether God will ever give you victory over your finances. If you are struggling under a heavy load of debt, you are in the middle of what may be your most important test ever.

I have not done an injustice by applying all three of these tests to your personal finances. These verses immediately follow a parable in which our Lord taught specifically on the subject of money.

"And he said also unto his disciples, There was a certain rich man, which had a steward; and the same was accused unto him that he had wasted his goods. And he called him, and said unto him, How is it that I hear this of thee? give an account of thy stewardship; for thou mayest be no longer steward. Then the steward said within himself, What shall I do? for my lord taketh away from me the stewardship: I cannot dig; to beg I am ashamed. I am resolved what to do, that, when I am put out of the stewardship, they may receive me into their houses. So he called every one of his lord's debtors unto him, and said unto the first, How much owest thou unto my lord? And he said, An hundred measures of oil. And he said unto him, Take thy bill, and sit down quickly, and write fifty. Then said he to another, And how much owest thou? And he said, An hundred measures of wheat. And he said unto him, Take thy bill, and write fourscore.

And the lord commended the unjust steward, because he had done wisely: for the children of this world are in their generation wiser than the children of light. And I say unto you, Make to yourselves friends of the mammon of unrighteousness; that, when ye fail, they may receive you into everlasting habitations." Luke 16:1-9

This is an amazing passage that is full of financial principles for God's people. I hope you took the time to read each word carefully. Remember that Jesus taught this parable as an explanation of God's three tests. Let's examine what God is teaching us here:

A rich man had a steward – The rich man represents God, and the steward is you. This is a parable that teaches about you, your God, and what you should do with His money.

The steward was accused – The accusation of the steward is given in the passive voice, taking the emphasis off of the accuser and directing us to focus on the accused. If you are failing financially, it will do no good looking for someone else to blame. The full responsibility falls on you to correct your own financial situation.

The steward had wasted his lord's goods – The steward had taken his lord's money and used it wastefully. The emphasis is not on what he did wrong, but on what he did not do that was right. We don't know what the steward did with his lord's money. We only know what he did NOT do. If you have not been a good steward, then you have also wasted your Lord's money.

The steward had a chance to redeem himself – If you are still breathing, it is not too late. At the same time, if you ignore the problem you may lose the chance to be a steward. Practically speaking, if you cannot show God that you will follow correct principles you could lose your money or even your life.

The steward found a solution – There will always be an answer. Eliminate what you absolutely cannot do. Whatever is left is what you must do. Take responsibility for yourself.

Notice that the steward was initially labeled as unjust, but later commended for behaving wisely. This distinction is crucial for understanding the point of Jesus' parable.

The steward prepared for the future – He was resigned that he would lose his stewardship, but he was determined to do what he could to make things better in the future. As quickly as possible, the steward used his lord's money to secure his future income. Do not waste your time lamenting over what you should have done last week, last month, or twenty years ago. Begin now. Use the money over which your Lord has given you authority to make sure you will have what you need in the future without having to work or beg.

The steward was wiser than the average Christian – He used his lord's money to take care of his and his family's short-term future. In other words, he used a percentage of the money over which he was steward to make sure his future was secure. His master commended him for this. Then Jesus directs His words to His audience and says that this man was wiser than the children of light.

Now, hold onto your seat! This might sting a little. While the steward was busy wasting the money over which he had been given authority, he was called unjust – which means that he was morally wrong. Yet when he took some of that same money as his own and used it to secure his future, he was commended and called wise.

How much of the money over which you have authority have you used to prepare for your future? When you reach the point where you are no longer able to do physical labor and you are too ashamed to beg, who will take care of you? Have you used the "unrighteous mammon" to prepare an "everlasting habitation"?

Have you been faithful in the little things?

Have you been faithful with your money?

Have you been faithful in that which belongs to someone else?

This parable has confused Bible students for centuries because they have tried to give it a solely spiritual application. They have struggled with the apparent discord between the rich man's praise and the steward's perceived dishonesty. I believe that Jesus gave us this parable to teach us a financial truth. All of our money belongs to God. God expects us to be a wise enough steward to use a portion of it to prepare for our own future. When the steward began using a percentage of the money under his authority to provide for a perpetual retirement, he was praised by his master.

Allow me to be brutally blunt. Much of what we call faith is ignorance or even stupidity. Many children of light take their paychecks and waste it on toys and trinkets that have no value to the kingdom of God. They then depend solely on the government to care for them in their old age, while claiming to live by faith. Finally they die, leaving nothing for their children.[3]

That is not living by faith! That is foolishness. It is wasteful, and it is morally wrong. These people are not being good stewards.

Many children of light have wasted their stewardships for generations, leaving themselves and their descendants dependent on Social Security and Medicare and unable to advance the Gospel and the Kingdom of God because of a lack of funds. They have forced their children to start with nothing.

If you have paid into Social Security for many years, then you are entitled to that income. At the same time you should not be dependent on it. How much better it would be to follow a plan that provides you with income at the end of your life that you can pass on to your children after you die.

Faith is obeying the commands and principles of God regardless of the perceived results. If God commended a previously unjust steward because he finally took matters into his own hands, and then slams the children of light who didn't have a clue, where does that leave us?

Perhaps it is time for you to follow the steward's example and to speak firmly to yourself. Try saying this:

I am God's steward. All of my money belongs to Him. I desire to be wise and not wasteful. As of today, I am determined to use a percentage of what God has given me to provide for the perpetual future of my family.

Details on how to achieve this will be given in Chapter 12.

[1] Proverbs 6:9-11
[2] Galatians 6:7
[3] Proverbs 19:14

MONEY IS NOT EVIL

"For the love of money is the root of all evil: which while some coveted after, they have erred from the faith, and pierced themselves through with many sorrows."   1 Timothy 6:10

The devil is a counterfeiter. He is an expert at taking the good things that God has given to us and changing them into something sinful. He often does this by offering those good things in the wrong way, in the wrong amount, or at the wrong time.

Music is a wonderful gift from God. The book of Psalms commands us to praise God with music.[1] When the beat of the music is emphasized more than the melody, however, that same music becomes a sensual tool that is used by the devil to excite the flesh.

Sleep is another wonderful gift from our Lord.[2] What can be more satisfying than climbing into bed at the end of a busy day? Yet the sin of slothfulness is the same thing taken to the extreme.

Food is another example. No one can live for long without eating, and one of the first things we will do in Heaven is to sit down and eat at the Marriage Supper of the Lamb.[3] But eating more than one's body needs is called gluttony in the Bible, and so we find that eating can also be sinful.[4]

The physical relationship between a man and a wife is one of the sweetest things that human beings can enjoy. When taken outside of the boundaries of marriage, however, this same act between a man and a woman draws a curse from God.[5]

Money is similar to these other gifts from God. Money in itself is not evil. Money is a tool given to us by God to live our lives and to accomplish His work.[6] Money allows us to tithe, to eat, to drive our cars, to buy a house, to get an education, or to enjoy a vacation. Money allows us to buy Bibles, to send missionaries to foreign lands, to print tracts, and to build church buildings.

In its right place, money is a good thing and a necessary thing. Money can even be one of the rewards that God gives us for doing right.[7] Money is not evil. It is the *love* of money that is a sin. This misdirected love is the root of all evil.

Just like food, sleep, intimacy, or music; money becomes sinful when taken out of its proper context. But used in the right way, money can do much for the Kingdom of God. It is crucial that you understand that money itself is not the issue, but rather how that money is used and the priority that it is given.

Before you learn the practical lessons on handling your money, you need to learn to think the right way about money. These early chapters are written to teach you the right thought processes.

First, you need to learn what money is. Before you can learn to correctly deal with your money, you must understand what you are dealing with.

WHAT IS MONEY?

Take out a dollar bill and place it in your hand. Can you eat it? Can you use it to shelter yourself from the rain? Can you heat your home with it? Can you ride it to work, to church, or to the mall? Can it turn on the lights? Can you put it into your gas tank in order to make your car run? Money cannot do any of these things, and yet it is practically impossible to live today without it.

MONEY IS AN IDEA

In the early days of America's history, most transactions were done by bartering. Bartering was difficult because it only worked when both people wanted what the other person had, both wanted to trade at the same time, and the value of the two items being traded was fairly equal. By the time the first European settlers arrived, the American Indians were already using wampum as a medium of exchange. This was America's first money.

The early settlers introduced gold and silver coins into society. Since these coins were much more portable than the goods themselves they made trading much easier, especially over large distances. Goods were bought and sold by exchanging coins of gold or silver equal to the value of the goods.

Today we buy and sell using colored pieces of paper with pictures of dead men to represent value. They are no longer connected to the value of a precious metal. The value of our money is decided by what our government tells us it is worth. What is the real difference between a one dollar bill and a one hundred dollar bill?

When visiting another country, those pieces of colored paper have to be exchanged for other pieces of colored paper that are worth whatever the government of that country says that they are worth. The only reason that anyone accepts these colored pieces of paper as money is because everyone accepts them.

People today are happy to be paid in $20 bills, even if they are just paper and ink. Someone living three hundred years ago would think that we were insane. We have even moved beyond that. A man's wages can now be paid directly into his bank account by computers. That same money can then be spent at the grocery store by using a debit card without the man ever actually seeing his money. We are able to walk into a store with empty hands and walk back out with a cart full of groceries, all because of this strange thing that we call money.

MONEY IS TIME

If a man's employer pays him $10 per hour, and he works for one hour, he has effectively traded one hour of his life for that $10. He gives up eight hours of his day to get $80, and the best part of his week to earn $400. In this sense, he is exchanging his life for that money. This is one reason why stealing is so evil. If someone were to steal $100 from this man, they would have literally stolen ten hours of his life.

As a man's abilities increase, his wages often increase as well. Because of his additional knowledge and skill, his time becomes more valuable. The more that you learn about money, the more you will see that wisdom and knowledge are worth more than any other abilities.

Those who receive money without working for it lose any sense of its worth. Because they have not sacrificed any time or effort to get the money, they have no way to measure its value. That is why those who live on money from the government are often the first to ask for another handout and often spend their money foolishly.

"For even when we were with you, this we commanded you, that if any would not work, neither should he eat."   2 Thessalonians 3:10

MONEY IS A TOOL

Although I cannot eat money, I can use it to buy food for my family. Although money cannot keep me warm, I can use it to buy gas or electricity that will keep me warm. Although money cannot shelter my family, it can rent or buy a house where they can be sheltered.

Money cannot save a soul, but it can pay for Bibles and Gospel tracts. It can purchase a church building and pay for the electricity to turn on the lights. It can buy pianos, songbooks, microphones and speakers, and pews to sit on.

Money cannot baptize a convert, but it can pay for a baptistery to be built. Money cannot do anything on its own, but it is an effective tool that can help get the job done. Money is a tool that lets you do more than you could do without it.

"And he said unto them, When I sent you without purse, and scrip, and shoes, lacked ye any thing? And they said, Nothing. Then said he unto them, But now, he that hath a purse, let him take it, and likewise his scrip: and he that hath no sword, let him sell his garment, and buy one."   Luke 22:35, 36

The first time that Jesus sent out His disciples, He commanded them to take nothing so they would learn that God would care for them. The second time He sent them out, Jesus commanded them to take the money that they would need to do the job. Jesus ordered His disciples to use money!

All Bible-believing Christians have been given a job to do. Every Bible-believing church has a responsibility to preach the Gospel to a lost world. Money cannot replace willing laborers, but it can make the job much easier for those who are willing to work. How many more people around the world would be reached with the Gospel if we had all of the money necessary to do the job?

MONEY IS A DEFENSE

Money allows me to be fruitful even during a calamity. If I have promised someone a ride to church next Sunday, having money ensures that I will be able to fulfill my commitment. I know that I can afford to get my car's engine repaired, replace the inspection sticker, pay for the registration, or put gas in the tank.

If one of my children gets sick and I have some money, I can afford to buy medicine. If I lose my job but I have some money, I know that my family will not starve.

"For wisdom is a defence, and money is a defence: but the excellency of knowledge is, that wisdom giveth life to them that have it." Ecclesiastes 7:12

Some Christians have been taught to give everything they have to the church. Some Christians have been taught that insurance is wrong. When these same Christians become widowed or disabled, their church and their pastor are rarely able to support them. Many people in America live paycheck to paycheck and are utterly devastated if something out of the ordinary occurs. Later in this book you will learn some ways that you can use your money to defend yourself against any difficulties that may arise.

"The rich man's wealth is his strong city: the destruction of the poor is their poverty."   Proverbs 10:15

MONEY IS OPPORTUNITY

If I have money, then I have more options available to me. If my family needs a vacation, then I have a number of choices of where we can go. If we need a new car, I can buy the one that best suits our needs. If there is a special offering being taken, then I can decide how much of a blessing I can be. If I see someone in need, then I have the opportunity to help. The more money that I have the more choices I can make.

Those who have much money have many choices.

Those who have little money have few choices.

Those who have no money have no choices.

When Joseph had to take his new bride and their son into Egypt to save the baby Jesus' life, he could not do it without money. Even in Bible days it cost money to travel, to buy food, and to stay in the inns along the way. As amazing a man as he was, Joseph still could not take time to stop and set up a carpenter's shop in order to earn a few shekels. It is wonderful to see how God sent some wise men to worship the young child and to give His parents some gifts. The first gift given was gold, and so Joseph had the ability to flee Herod's persecution and to save the Messiah.[8]

Money itself is not evil. It is not wrong to have it or even to want it. It is very wrong to love it. We must use money with the right heart attitude. When a man falls in love with money, his misplaced desires will cause him to do evil to get it. Thus the love of money is the root of all evil, while having money gives you the opportunity to do good for yourself and for others.

[1] Psalm 150:3-5

[2] Psalm 127:2
[3] Revelation 19:9
[4] Proverbs 23:21
[5] Hebrews 13:4
[6] James 1:17
[7] Proverbs 22:4
[8] Matthew 2:11

THE KEY INGREDIENT

There is one key ingredient that must be a part of all of your financial dealings. Without this one ingredient, you are bound to fail. It is no exaggeration to say that it is the most important thing that you can ever have in your dealings with money. This crucial ingredient is called integrity.

Integrity is so necessary that if you should ever be forced to choose between having integrity and having money, you must always choose integrity. Money that is lost can be regained. Integrity that is lost is lost forever.

"Better is the poor that walketh in his integrity, than he that is perverse in his lips, and is a fool."   Proverbs 19:1

What is integrity? Integrity is being true to your word. It is fair and honest dealing. It is avoiding the least shade of dishonesty. It is doing what is legal, but also doing what is ethical. It is living right. It is never cutting corners. It is being above reproach. Integrity is doing unto others what you would have them do unto you.

Throughout your lifetime you will deal with many different types of people. When you find that you are dealing with a person of integrity, you will have found a treasure. When that person finds that they are also dealing with a person of integrity that is an even greater treasure.

You may get rich by being a crook, but you will still be a crook. You may get ahead for a while by climbing over top of others, but you will continually have to find new victims to deceive.

If you find that you are working with someone who does not have integrity, stop immediately and walk away. A man who has integrity will eventually gather around him a group of similarly minded people with whom he has built a bond of trust. These people will often work together their whole lives.

In 2 Samuel 5, Hiram the king of Tyre began business dealings with King David. David found that Hiram was a man of integrity, and David's kingdom was blessed when he dealt with Hiram.

In 1 Kings 5, Solomon also dealt with Hiram. Because Hiram had proven his integrity, Solomon had no need to take his business elsewhere. Both kingdoms flourished as a result of the relationship.

INTEGRITY WILL MAKE MANY DECISIONS FOR YOU

In the world of finance, one decision may help you or hurt you for a long time. Occasionally, you will need to make a decision within a set time or lose an opportunity. When you are in one of these situations, your decision will often be made for you by your integrity. You will have a built-in guide to lead you in the right way.

"The integrity of the upright shall guide them: but the perverseness of transgressors shall destroy them."   Proverbs 11:3

If you are asked to do something shady to make a deal happen, don't do it. If you are tempted to hide something from the police or from the Internal Revenue Service, don't do it. If you have to cheat, hurt, or take advantage of someone, don't do it. If you are asked to do something that would bring reproach upon your parents, your family, your church, or the Lord, don't do it.

If it is not ethical, don't do it. If there is anything questionable about it, don't do it. If you don't understand it, don't do it. If you don't like anything about the deal, just walk away. You must absolutely refuse to compromise in any way in order to make money. Your integrity must never be for sale.

INTEGRITY WILL PROTECT YOU FROM SCAMS

In recent years many people have been caught in scams. Even today, they are still being deceived by overseas tax havens and by emails from Nigerian princesses.

These deceptive deals appeal to those who think that there must be a secret way to get rich. They hint that you may be able to do it without paying taxes or that you can get money away from someone who is more foolish than you are.

No one ever needs to be dishonest to make money! There are too many honest ways to earn it. A man of integrity will shy away from anything questionable and, in so doing, will protect himself from destruction.

"Let integrity and uprightness preserve me; for I wait on thee."
Psalm 25:21

INTEGRITY WILL KEEP YOU IN GOD'S GOOD GRACES

King Abimelech made a mistake in Genesis 20. In ignorance he took Abraham's wife, Sarah, planning to make her his own wife. When God called him to task, Abimelech's only defense was his integrity.

King Abimelech was trying to keep everything honest and aboveboard. He had not intended to do anything wrong. God acknowledged Abimelech's integrity and then forgave him any punishment because of it.

Even after you have learned everything that you can about finances, you will still make mistakes. When you do, you better have God smiling at you. Here is a truth that everyone needs to tattoo on their brain:

You cannot succeed if God is not pleased!

"And as for me, thou upholdest me in mine integrity, and settest me before thy face for ever." Psalm 41:12

King David was a man after God's own heart. David was also a man who walked in integrity. David was by no means perfect, but God blessed him bountifully.

"And if thou wilt walk before me, as David thy father walked, in integrity of heart, and in uprightness, to do according to all that I have commanded thee, and wilt keep my statutes and my judgments:" 1 Kings 9:4

INTEGRITY WILL BRING YOU MORE OPPORTUNITIES

This may come as a shock to you, but there are people in this world who are looking to give you money. That's right! They want to hand you their cash. Those people who have an excess of money are continually looking for good investments. It is never difficult to find a new idea or a new company in which to invest, but it is often difficult to find someone who can be trusted.

Once the business people of this world learn that you have integrity, the doors of possibility will open wide. Once you have gained their trust you will not have to ask for money. They will try to give it to you. Good deals will come your way. Your integrity is valuable to these people. Do not be surprised when they begin to call you.

YOUR INTEGRITY WILL LAST LONG AFTER YOU ARE GONE

When you transact all of your business dealings with integrity, you will leave behind a reputation that will bless your children. Just as a parent's sin will visit the third and fourth generations, so a man's integrity will do the same. This is part of the heritage that you are building for your descendants.

"The just man walketh in his integrity: his children are blessed after him." Proverbs 20:7

We saw that Job was rich and spiritual, then poor and spiritual, then rich and spiritual again. The reason Job had the opportunity to regain his wealth was because he never lost his integrity.

"God forbid that I should justify you: till I die I will not remove mine integrity from me." Job 27:5

You must decide that you will be absolutely correct in all that you do with your money. Every transaction, every agreement, every contract, and every decision must be completely above reproach. You will never succeed in the area of finances by taking advantage of someone. Every move must assure trust in you.

"A good name is rather to be chosen than great riches, and loving favour rather than silver and gold." Proverbs 22:1

Paul had integrity when it came to the money that was entrusted to him as he made his missionary journeys. He was a good steward.

"Providing for honest things, not only in the sight of the Lord, but also in the sight of men." 2 Corinthians 8:21

"Recompense to no man evil for evil. Provide things honest in the sight of all men." Romans 12:17

ONLY THE BY-PRODUCT

While reading my Bible one morning, I found what seemed to me to be a contradiction. I firmly believe that God cannot contradict Himself, and that any perceived contradiction in the Bible is simply my human misunderstanding. Therefore I knew that I was missing something. One of the verses that I read, however, appeared very positive about money while the other appeared very negative. The more I thought about it, the more confused that I became. How could I reconcile Proverbs 22:4, *"By humility and the fear of the LORD are riches, and honour, and life,"* with 1 Timothy 6:10a, *"For the love of money is the root of all evil:"*?

In order to understand better what God was trying to tell me, I decided to list every verse in the book of Proverbs dealing with finances. As you have already read, I found 159 verses that deal directly with money as well as many others that do not specifically mention finances but that contain principles that can readily be applied to all of our financial dealings.

I began putting these verses into two columns with the first column containing all the verses that spoke positively about money, and the second column containing all the verses that spoke negatively about money. As I carried out this exercise, things began to fall into place.

The first thing I noticed was that those verses with a positive outlook were not speaking positively about the money itself, but about the person involved. Money is just the by-product of that man or woman doing what God says is right.

The second thing I noticed was that those verses with a negative outlook were not speaking negatively about the money either. Again, the verses were referring to the person involved. After finishing the entire exercise, I came to the realization that money is neither good nor evil, neither positive nor negative, neither right nor wrong. It is you or I that take the moral position, and what we do with our money simply exposes us for what we are.

Perhaps this illustration will help you to understand better. Imagine two athletes who decide to play tennis. The first player is an honest, ethical man who desires to be the best tennis player that he can be. As he proceeds from game to game, from set to set, he strives to make each shot perfectly. He concentrates on his serve, his stance, his grip, his swing, and his follow-through. He reads books about tennis, he takes lessons, and he studies the pros. He does the best that he can with the equipment that he has, and he finishes each match knowing he has done his best and with a sincere desire to do better tomorrow.

The second man is a liar and a cheat. His goal is just to win. In order to do this, he hits the ball when the other player is not ready. He lies about the score. He deliberately attempts to damage the other player's equipment and tries to cause him harm. He calls his shots in when they are out and the other player's shots out when they are in. He finishes the game with the most points and claims the victory.

Over time the first man will continue to improve his tennis game with the natural result being that he gains more points as he gains experience. The second man will eventually be discovered as the cheater that he is, and then no other tennis players will want to play with him. At first he may finish with the most points, but over time his reputation will be ruined. The goal of tennis is not just to get the most points. The real goal is to be the best tennis player that you can be. Points and victories are only the by-products of hard work and practice.

The same principle applies to money. The wise man or woman will strive to handle their money in a way that pleases the Lord and will continually be looking for ways to improve their "game." They will respect their partners, do the best they can with what they have, and will maintain an attitude of good sportsmanship. As a result, they will gain more points *(dollars)*, and other players will enjoy their company. They will become better players and the true winners. A good steward is rewarded with more stewardship.

Likewise, the foolish man or woman is only concerned with the points. This is the "love of money," which is the "root of all evil." They do not hesitate to take advantage of everyone they can in order to get ahead. As a result, they have a harder and harder time finding anyone who will play with them and eventually cannot get any points because they are out of the game and possibly in jail.

The purpose of this chapter is to help you to see that money is not good or bad. The issue is not the points. The issue is how you are playing the game. Once you have that principle clear in your mind, you are ready to go on to the next step. Before you read any further in this book, you need to be willing to commit that your goal is to be the best player that you can possibly be, and that you will allow the money to simply be the by-product of your goal.

I am willing to commit that my goal is to be the best financial player that I can possibly be, and that I will allow money to simply be the by-product of my goal.

Your signature

Now let's look at the Bible plan for improving. The Bible teaches you certain things that must be a part of your life. Introducing these good and right traits into your financial life will make you a better Christian as well as a better player in the game of money. They will also eventually result in you having more money.

"By humility and the fear of the LORD are riches, and honour, and life." Proverbs 22:4

FEAR THE LORD

This is an important requirement in every saved person's life. We are supposed to fear the Lord the same way that a child fears a loving parent. The child is not afraid of their parent, but they fear the results of disobeying their parent.

In other words, we know that our God is a loving God but we fear what He could do if we step outside of His boundaries. When God sees a person that fears Him, He knows that He can trust them with more. They will then receive more riches.

For a man to try to gain riches outside of fearing God is folly. What good would it do to have a lot of money if God is displeased with you? The fear of the Lord is the goal, and money is the by-product.

"Better is little with the fear of the LORD than great treasure and trouble therewith." Proverbs 15:16

STAY HUMBLE

As your wealth begins to grow, you must purposely avoid pride. Remind yourself regularly that you could not earn a single dollar without God's help. You cannot even breathe without His permission. Remind yourself regularly that having money never made anyone a better person. Never allow yourself to look down on someone because they have less money than you do.

Do not get proud. Do not fight God in this matter. As long as you stay humble, God is free to continue to bless you. If you begin to get proud, God is bound by His Word to humble you. You could say it this way: *"I must keep myself humble. If I do not keep myself humble, then God surely will."* Humility is the goal, and money is the by-product.

"For whosoever exalteth himself shall be abased; and he that humbleth himself shall be exalted." Luke 14:11

"Humble yourselves in the sight of the Lord, and he shall lift you up."
James 4:10

"Charge them that are rich in this world, that they be not highminded, nor trust in uncertain riches, but in the living God, who giveth us richly all things to enjoy;" 1 Timothy 6:17

SEEK KNOWLEDGE AND UNDERSTANDING

Some people who willingly invest thousands of dollars to follow another person's advice will balk at spending fifteen dollars on a book to learn how to do it themselves. Rather than learning how to invest, they will hand over their money and hope for the best. While it may be a good idea to ask someone to help you steward your money, you still need to know and understand what they are doing with it!

We are continuously commanded in the book of Proverbs to seek three things: wisdom, knowledge, and understanding.[1] You should seek knowledge in the area of money! The result of knowing and understanding something other people do not know or understand, but wish they did, is that you get money. Knowledge is the goal, and money is the by-product.

The prodigal son wanted his share of his father's wealth, but he did not have the knowledge necessary to handle it. As a result he was soon ready to eat pig food. Joseph sat in a prison cell with nothing but the shirt on his back, but because of his knowledge and understanding he was quickly promoted to a position of power.

"Riches and honour are with me; yea, durable riches and righteousness. My fruit is better than gold, yea, than fine gold; and my revenue than choice silver. I lead in the way of righteousness, in the midst of the paths of judgment: That I may cause those that love me to inherit substance; and I will fill their treasures."
Proverbs 8:18-21

ALWAYS SEEK TO HELP OTHERS

Some people are selfish, short-sighted, greedy, and needy. Many people are impatient and unwilling to learn. The person who chooses a life of service will find many willing recipients. Regardless of your occupation, if you use your life to make other people's lives better, then riches are the inevitable result.

When the first automobile was invented, it was only affordable by the very rich. Henry Ford developed the assembly line and made his Model T automobiles affordable for nearly everyone. As a result he became wealthy.

As computers became more popular and more useful, people wanted them in their homes. When a college dropout named Michael Dell contrived a way to sell cheap computers built on demand, he quickly became a multi-millionaire. Once people had these cheap computers in their homes they wanted to use them, but very few were willing or able to make the effort to learn computer code. Bill Gates became the wealthiest man in the world when he marketed a way to tell computers what to do by clicking on pictures on the screen.

Many people would like to invest in the stock market but do not want to take the time to understand it, so they pay someone else to invest their money for them. Presently, one of the most successful men in the world at investing other people's money for them is Warren Buffett. It is no coincidence that he is also the world's wealthiest investor.

Our world is desperate for servants. If you can find a way to serve others, then money will be a by-product. You may not see the result immediately, but the more successful you are at helping people, the more money will come your way. I encourage every young person to immediately start looking for ways to serve others.

Throughout the years of His public ministry, Jesus lived the life of a servant. He trained His disciples to be servants. As a result, He had a group of friends who followed Him around and fed Him, sheltered Him, and served Him.[2] We have no record that He ever sought these people, but they came as a natural result of His helping others.

When you go to your job tomorrow, do not spend your time concentrating on how much you will make per hour or how much time you have left before you can go home.

Instead, concentrate on how you can be more useful. Look for those tasks that others avoid, and volunteer to do them. If things are slow, ask your supervisor if there is anything that you can do in addition to your regular work. Since many people are trying to do as little as possible, your efforts will stand out. When pay raises and promotions come around, or when lay-offs become necessary, your efforts will be remembered. Service is the goal, and money is the by-product.

[1] Proverbs 16:16
[2] Luke 8:3

Your Financial State

The previous six chapters have been written for the purpose of helping you to think correctly about your money. Beginning with this chapter, you will learn the practical applications of the previous six chapters. Before you can begin to improve your financial situation, however, you must get a complete picture of where you are today.

"Be thou diligent to know the state of thy flocks, and look well to thy herds. For riches are not for ever: and doth the crown endure to every generation? The hay appeareth, and the tender grass sheweth itself, and herbs of the mountains are gathered. The lambs are for thy clothing, and the goats are the price of the field. And thou shalt have goats' milk enough for thy food, for the food of thy household, and for the maintenance for thy maidens."
Proverbs 27:23-27

In this lesson you are going to learn how to discern your present financial situation. This should not be a one-time exercise. Notice that the Bible commands you to be diligent in knowing your financial state. Although in Bible times wealth was measured by the number of animals someone owned and today it is measured by how much money someone has, the principles remain the same. This exercise ought to be diligently repeated at regular intervals throughout your life. Imagine it as the difference between a single photograph and a video. Regularly repeating this exercise will allow you to see the progress you are making with your finances.

You will need some paper and a pen. You are going to divide your finances into five different categories. These categories are:

Income
Bills
Debts
Possessions
Assets

INCOME

For this exercise, income is the amount of money that you know you will receive on a regular basis. Income would include your salary, wages, Social Security, benefits, pensions, rental income, royalties, interest, dividends, etc. If this amount varies greatly from week to week or from month to month, then write down the most conservative figure. At this point you should not include irregular income such as overtime, bonuses, commissions, gifts, inheritances, or tax returns.

You need to determine the amount of income that you know you will receive each month. For most people a monthly amount is the easiest to determine, and that figure will correspond with their bills that need to be paid on a monthly basis. For the remainder of this book, we will assume a monthly time period for all of our calculations.

If you are paid weekly, simply multiply the amount of your income by 52 weeks and divide by 12 months. If you are paid bi-weekly, multiply that amount by 26 and divide by 12. The result will be your regular monthly income.

In two columns list your different sources of regular income along with the monthly amount that you receive from each one. You may want to use Worksheet 1 found in the appendix.

BILLS

Your bills are defined as those obligations that you will be paying for all of your foreseeable future. Most people will be paying an electric bill for the rest of their lives. Barring unusual circumstances, you will probably pay a telephone bill until the day you die. Your most important bill, and the bill that you should pay first every month, is your rent for living on God's planet. This is called your tithe. You will be paying your tithe for the rest of the time you live here on earth.

Some examples of your bills are your tithe, income taxes, Social Security, state taxes, insurances, electric, gas, water, phone, internet, cable, regular medication, missions giving, charities, etc. If you are renting, you would include your rent here. Include your monthly mortgage payment here if you have more than five years left to pay.

These are all considered bills because they need to be paid regularly, and except for the mortgage, they will never be finished. A new bill will show up every month. Do not include car payments, credit cards, or short term loans in this section.

In two columns list all of the bills that you pay each month along with the monthly amount that you normally pay for each one. If any bill, such as your electric bill, fluctuates through the year use the average for the past twelve months. Worksheet 2 is provided in the appendix to help you with categorizing your bills.

DEBTS

Your debts are those bills that have an end date. No matter how impossible it may seem right now, there is light at the end of the tunnel. Your debts include all credit card balances, car payments, personal loans, bank loans, medical bills, student loans, money borrowed from friends and family, etc. You should also include any mortgage with less than five years to pay. You must be absolutely honest with yourself here. Write down every dollar that you owe to everyone, everywhere. Go back and dig up those debts that you have shoved in the back of the hopeless drawer. You are going to learn how to pay them all back.

In four columns list all of your debts along with the total amount that you still have to pay for each one, the minimum monthly payment, and the interest rate you are paying on each debt. Carefully completing Worksheet 3 found in the appendix will give an overall view of your debt and will also be very helpful when you get to Chapters 10 and 11.

POSSESSIONS

Your possessions are all of your material goods. This includes things such as your house, vehicles, furniture, appliances, electronics, computers, clothing, tools, jewelry, china, silver, sports equipment, artwork, books, coins, stamps, baseball cards, etc. You can further divide this group into two smaller categories: *Goods* and *Treasures*.

Goods are things that you use often, or at least occasionally, such as your clothes, furniture, appliances, and tools. If you had to sell these things you would recoup some of the purchase price but you would probably not get back what you paid for them. In most cases you would also have to buy something else to replace them.

Treasures are those things that you are saving because you hope to sell them someday for a profit, or that you are holding because of inherent or sentimental value.

List all of your possessions in one column, and write down in a second column how much you would get if you sold them. Use Worksheet 4 in the appendix if it helps.

Refrain from being too optimistic with this list. It is easy to choose a number that makes you feel good but is not realistic. Take time to do some research and find an accurate number. Be sure to check on some online auction sites or enquire with a broker to get other's opinions of what your possessions are worth.

I suggest that you take pictures of all your belongings while making this inventory. These photos will be helpful in dealing with your insurance company should that ever become necessary.

This process may also bring to your attention how much you own that you do not use. If you have not used something for more than six months, you probably never will. It may be a good idea to sell it and use the money for something more profitable. You will learn more about that in a later chapter.

ASSETS

These are the things that you own which are currently earning you money. They are adding to your income. This list would include interest bearing savings accounts, investments, rental properties, home businesses, royalty rights, dividend-paying stocks, bonds, annuities, etc.

You can include in this list anything that helps you make money, as long as you can attribute a definite amount of income. Do not include anything in this list unless it is presently producing income.

Worksheet 5, found in the appendix, will help you to get a good picture of your income-producing assets. This worksheet in particular is very sobering for most people because it is left blank!

DETERMINING YOUR FINANCIAL STATE

Write the following information on a separate piece of paper:
1. How often you get paid (weekly, every two weeks, monthly)
2. Your total income each month
3. Your total bills each month
4. Your total debts
5. Your total minimum monthly payment of debts

First, add the total amount of your bills to the total minimum payments of your debts for each month. Then subtract that total from your total income for the same time frame.

Total Income - (Total Bills + Total Minimum Payments) =

In accounting terms, this is known as a Cash Flow Statement. It shows how your cash flows in and out. You should complete a Cash Flow Statement at least once every six months. Worksheet 6 in the appendix will simplify this exercise.

Now make a list of everything that you own, along with an amount of its worth. Do not put down the amount that you paid for each item. Instead, write down the amount that you would receive if you were to sell each item. Again, be honest with yourself. You may have paid $1,000 for a plush leather armchair, but if the springs are sprung and the leather is torn, it is probably worth very little today.

For large items such as your house and car, some time on the internet should help you to find a fairly accurate value. The important thing is to write down what you would actually get for selling it, not what you hope or wish you would get.

Last, make a list of everything you owe and to whom it is owed. Subtract the total of what you owe from the total of what you own to find your net worth. Hopefully you will arrive at a positive number. If the final number is negative, do not give up hope. This is an ongoing process. In later chapters you will learn how to improve your net worth.

Total of what I own – Total of what I owe =

In accounting terms, this is known as a Balance Sheet. It shows the balance of what you own against what you owe. You should complete a Balance Sheet at least once every six months. Worksheet 7 in the appendix will make this easy.

"Wherefore do ye spend money for that which is not bread? and your labour for that which satisfieth not? hearken diligently unto me, and eat ye that which is good, and let your soul delight itself in fatness."   Isaiah 55:2

"He becometh poor that dealeth with a slack hand: but the hand of the diligent maketh rich."   Proverbs 10:4

A Budget that Works

For many people, the word "budget" has a nasty connotation. You may have sat down at some time in the past and categorized your spending and income with the hope that you would be able to solve all of your financial problems.

If you are like most people, you were not successful. The problem with most budgets is that they are too complicated, they are too confining, and they just don't work.

With the average budget, you write down all of the different categories where you spend money and then designate a certain amount to be spent from that category each month.

The first difficulty arises when your electric bill is $212.72 and you only budgeted $200.00. Then you need $167.43 for groceries when your budget only allows you $150.00. You borrow from your clothing account because you didn't use the $20.00 that is in there, but the next week your child needs new shoes that cost $39.95.

After a few months of doing this you throw the whole thing out the window, proclaim that budgets don't work, and slowly drift back into financial misery.

The problem with these types of budgets is that they are too constraining for real life. In the midst of the frustration caused by these impractical budgets, many people decide that all budgets are useless. You need a budget that you can use, but that is much more suited to the way that you live. You need a budget that works.

This may be the most important chapter of this book as far as the practical handling of your money. In this chapter you are going to learn how to set up a new type of budget that you can really use.

You are going to do this by learning and using two Biblical principles: **Percentages** and **Priorities**.

BUDGETING BY PERCENTAGES

When God gave Moses the civil laws for ruling the nation of Israel, He included in those laws all of the fines and taxes that the Israelites would have to pay. A few of these taxes were a set amount. For example, the tabernacle tax was just one half of a shekel.[1] It did not matter whether someone was rich or poor; everyone above the age of twenty paid the same amount.

For most of these taxes and fines, however, the amount that you paid was decided by a percentage. If a thief stole something, he had to repay what he had taken plus an additional 20% as a fine.[2] If a man redeemed a vow or any of his tithes, he was to add the fifth part to it.[3] Again, that is 20%.

The tithe, of course, was 10%. When the Levites tithed on the tithes that they received from the people of Israel they gave the Lord their tenth from that tenth.[4]

When Joseph was placed in charge of Egypt's harvest, he set the tax rate at one-fifth or 20%.[5] It did not matter if someone was a pauper or a millionaire, they paid the same percentage. Today we would call this a straight-line income tax or a flat-rate tax.

The budget that you should be using is not a budget of set amounts, but rather a budget that is set by percentages. As your income changes the size of the amounts will change with it, but the percentages will always stay the same.

No matter what your financial situation is today, the percentage of your tithe will always be exactly the same as everyone else. The percentage that you save will be the same. The percentage that you will use to pay off your debts will be the same.

Throughout your life your income may vary, but using these percentages will help you to keep things simple. You can start using this budget today.

BUDGETING BY PRIORITIES

The second Biblical principle is that of paying for your most important obligations first. In other words, you should not take your paycheck and immediately run out and buy everything you saw in the latest department store flyer. Have you ever noticed that those flyers seem to arrive in your mailbox just before you get paid?

With your new budget, you will determine those obligations that you are spiritually, morally, and ethically obligated to pay first. These will receive priority in descending order. When using this budget you will no longer spend your money for things depending on how much you want them, but you will instead learn to spend your money according to what is right.

As you follow God's principles your finances will fall into place, and you will find that you have the money to buy the things that you need. You are becoming a good steward!

A BUDGET THAT WORKS

Sit down with your last paycheck stub, a calculator, a pen and some paper. You now need to make some simple calculations using the percentages and the priorities that will decide how you are going to spend your – and God's – money.

Pay your tithe
Percentage: 10%
Priority: Always first

Find the number on your paystub that represents your gross income. Write that number down. Then add any other income that you have received throughout the past month. Make sure to include every dollar. Add all overtime, bonuses, birthday or Christmas gifts, found money, housing allowances, tax returns, and any other income. Write down the total of all of these and then divide it by ten. You can use your calculator to find this number.

A simple shortcut is to write down the figure and move the decimal point one space to the left. Then round up to the next full cent.

> Total income = $ 987.50   Tithe = $ 98.75
> Total income = $ 314.00   Tithe = $ 31.40
> Total income = $2,567.45   Tithe = $256.75

Always pay your tithe to your local church as soon as you can after receiving your pay. This would normally be the following Sunday.[6]

"Honour the LORD with thy substance, and with the firstfruits of all thine increase: So shall thy barns be filled with plenty, and thy presses shall burst out with new wine."   Proverbs 3:9, 10

"Bring ye all the tithes into the storehouse, that there may be meat in mine house, and prove me now herewith, saith the LORD of hosts, if I will not open you the windows of heaven, and pour you out a blessing, that there shall not be room enough to receive it."
                                                                    Malachi 3:10

Pay your debts
Percentage: 10%
Priority: Second

Your debts are those amounts that you have agreed to pay over time. We will go into more depth about this subject in Chapters 9 and 10, but for now your debts are not defined as the total amounts that you will repay.

Your debts are defined as the amounts that you owe right now. These amounts are commonly called your minimum payments.

Gather together your latest statements for each of the debts that you owe. On a separate piece of paper, write the minimum amount that you must pay every month next to the name of each debt. Then total all of your minimum payments. You may want to use Worksheet 8 found in the appendix.

If your minimum payments total less than 10% of your total income, you are in a good position financially. But even if your minimum payments are less than 10% of your income, you are not going to lower the percentage that you are using to pay off your debts. Instead, you are going to pay more than the minimum payment in order to pay off your debts sooner. You will continue to use 10% of your income to pay off your debts until they are gone.

Example: *If the total of your minimum payments is $550 per month, and 10% of your income is $700, then you are going to pay an extra $150 on one of your bills each month. You will be amazed how much quicker your debts will be paid off. This procedure will be explained in more detail in Chapter 10.*

If your minimum payments total more than 10% of your total income, then you will have to use more than 10% of your income. You need to continue making all of the minimum payments.

The reason that this is such a high priority is because the debt collection agencies will come looking for you if they are not paid. When you signed the documents stating that you would pay back these debts, you gave your word. Your integrity is at risk. Remember that your integrity is the key ingredient in all of your financial dealings. You must always pay all of the minimum payments of your debts.

Example: *If the total of your minimum payments is $700 per month, and 10% of your income is $550, then you are going to pay $700 per month even though it is more than 10% of your income.*

Pay your savings
Percentage: 10%
Priority: Third

You should be getting accustomed to using the same percentage. The same amount you calculated for your tithe is the same amount that you used to pay the minimum payments on your debts.

Now this same amount is going to be put into savings. Once you have paid your debt to God and others, you must pay yourself.

Please don't start making excuses just yet. You may think you can't make ends meet now. You may think you can't afford to save. You may think there is no extra money. Don't give up yet! Later in this book you are going to learn how, with some extra effort, you can easily save 10% of your income every month.

Right now the important thing is for you to have a savings account. This must be a separate account from your everyday checking or debit account. You may be able to set up an automatic transfer so that the 10% comes out of your regular account and goes into your savings account the same night your paycheck goes in.

This is the method the government uses to make sure that they get your tax money. They take it before you see it. You need to be just as strict with yourself as the government is with your tax money.

This steady stream of 10% saving is going to give you financial freedom in your future years and provide your children with an inheritance.

If the minimum payments of all your debts total more than 10%, you will take the difference out of your savings. For example, if the total of your minimum payments equals 13% of your income, then the amount that you put into savings will be 7% of your income. As the total amount of your debt decreases, you will be able to increase the amount that you put into savings.

Eventually you will have all of your debts paid off, and you will not have any money going towards minimum payments. When this happens you will have a choice for this money. Of course, you could spend it. After all, it is your money. You could also take the money that you have been using to pay off your debts and add it to the amount that you put into your savings until your savings equals 20% of your income. In the long run this will be a better choice.

The percentage of your tithe, debt payments, and savings should always total 20% to 30% of your total income. You will always give 10% of your income as your tithe. Then, once your debts are all paid you can put 10% to 20% of your income into your savings.

Pay your bills
Percentage: Varies
Priority: Fourth

With the remaining 70% of your income, you are going to pay all of your bills. This includes your groceries, electric bill, car payment, telephone bill, Faith Promise Missions pledge, medications, etc. Force yourself to write out the check or make the payment as soon as the money comes in. Do not put the remaining 70% of your income in your wallet or your purse with good intentions to pay your bills. Pay them right away. They are a higher priority than that new and shiny gadget or toy that is on sale for one day only.

Enjoy life
Percentage: Whatever is left
Priority: Last

Now you may go out to eat, buy that new outfit, give to the needy, or take a vacation. That's right! If you have paid your tithe, made all of your minimum payments, saved 10%, and paid your bills, then you are free to enjoy life. Whatever is left is really yours!

"Charge them that are rich in this world, that they be not highminded, nor trust in uncertain riches, but in the living God, who giveth us richly all things to enjoy;"   1 Timothy 6:17

Some people have lived in debt for so long that they have a continual voice in the back of their heads telling them that their money is not really theirs. For them, having money equals guilt. For some people it seems that anyone who has money to spend must have done something dishonest to get it. You may be one of those who have learned to think this way.

If you have money that is under no obligation, go ahead and enjoy it! God demands His 10%. Your integrity demands that you fulfill your obligations. Good stewardship demands that you prepare for your future. But God has given us this life to enjoy. After you have met your obligations, go ahead and have some fun!

"The thief cometh not, but for to steal, and to kill, and to destroy: I am come that they might have life, and that they might have it more abundantly." John 10:10

When completing these calculations, you should always determine 10% of your **gross** income when determining your tithe, but you may choose to use 10% of your net income when determining the amount you will use to pay your debts and to put into savings. You may also decide to put more than 10% into savings if your debt payments total less that 10% of your income.

SOME PRACTICAL EXAMPLES

Suppose that a single young man makes $600 per week. His gross monthly income would be $2,600. ($600 multiplied by 52 weeks and then divided by 12 months) This level of income would place him in the 15% tax bracket, meaning that he would pay $390 per month in taxes. His net monthly income would be $2,210.

Each month this young man should tithe $260. Another $260 would be used to pay off his debts. Another $260 would be automatically deposited into his savings account. He will then have $1,430 remaining with which to pay his bills and to enjoy life. If he chooses to use 10% of his **net** income, he would still tithe $260, but he would only put $221 towards both savings and debt repayment. He would then have $1,508 to pay his bills and to enjoy life.

If this same young man had no debts he would tithe $260. Then he could choose whether to base the percentage for his savings off of his gross income or his net income and whether to pay 10% or 20% toward savings.

A Budget that Works

Suppose the next month he receives the same pay, but he earns an additional $100 by working for a neighbor for a total of $2,700. This month the young man would pay $405 in taxes. He would tithe $270. Another $270 would be automatically deposited into his savings account. Another $270 would be used to pay off his debts. He will then have $1,485 remaining after taxes with which to pay his bills and to enjoy life. If he chooses to use 10% of his net income he would still tithe $270 but he would only put $230 towards debt repayment and $230 toward savings.

Now suppose that a middle aged couple brings in a combined monthly salary of $7,000. This level of income would place them in the 25% tax bracket, meaning that they would pay $1,750 per month in taxes. Their monthly net income would be $5,250.

Each month this couple should tithe $700. Another $700 would be used to pay off their debts. Another $700 would be automatically deposited into their savings account. They will then have $3,150 remaining after taxes with which to pay their bills and to enjoy life. If they choose to use 10% of their net income they would still tithe $700 but they would only put $525 toward savings and $525 toward debt repayment, leaving $3,500 to pay bills and enjoy.

[1] Exodus 30:12-15
[2] Leviticus 6:1-5
[3] Leviticus 27:9-15, 32
[4] Numbers 18:24-26
[5] Genesis 41:34; 47:24
[6] 1 Corinthians 16:2

Please note that the amounts and percentages given in these examples are only intended to clarify the illustrations. They should not be taken as financial advice. Tax rates may change annually.

WHAT IS THE TITHE?

If you have already surrendered to the principle of tithing, this will be a very simple chapter for you to understand and accept. If you have not yet yielded to the Bible's teaching in this area, please give me your heart as I teach this crucial doctrine to you.

It has sometimes been said that tithing is under the Mosaic Law. I will not discuss the motives of those that teach this, but I do want to show you that tithing is not confined to one part of history.

Tithing is found throughout the Bible. The first record of tithing is only fourteen chapters into the book of Genesis when Abram gave tithes to Melchizedek. The last Bible reference is found in the book of Hebrews, where tithing is mentioned with every indication that it is still important and necessary. The Lord Jesus Christ also spoke of tithing and commanded His disciples not to leave it undone.

"And he blessed him, and said, Blessed be Abram of the most high God, possessor of heaven and earth: And blessed be the most high God, which hath delivered thine enemies into thy hand. And he gave him tithes of all." Genesis 14:19, 20

"And here men that die receive tithes; but there he receiveth them, of whom it is witnessed that he liveth." Hebrews 7:8

"But woe unto you, Pharisees! for ye tithe mint and rue and all manner of herbs, and pass over judgment and the love of God: these ought ye to have done, and not to leave the other undone."
Luke 11:42

YOUR TITHE SHOWS THAT GOD IS FIRST IN YOUR LIFE

When Jacob was fleeing for his life from his angry brother, he stopped for the night somewhere between Beersheba and Haran. He slept with stones for a pillow and dreamed of a ladder reaching to Heaven with angels ascending and descending on it.

In Jacob's dream God promised to bless him and his descendants. When Jacob awoke, he made a vow that God would be his God. As an outward symbol of this decision, Jacob also promised to give God one-tenth of all his possessions.

"And this stone, which I have set for a pillar, shall be God's house: and of all that thou shalt give me I will surely give the tenth unto thee." Genesis 28:22

Throughout the Word of God, when men and women who were away from God made the decision to get back into His good graces, they began tithing. The Israelites began to tithe as soon as they came out of slavery in Egypt.[1] During the revival that began in Hezekiah's reign, the people began to tithe again.[2] So did the Jews who returned to Jerusalem with Nehemiah.[3] The prophets Amos and Malachi both preached tithing as a means of getting right with God.[4]

YOUR TITHE PASSES GOD'S TEST OF FAITH

Everything that we have comes from God and ought to be used to honor Him. But God also wants us to trust Him, and so He commands us to give back 10% of what He gives us. If we pass this test, then God will open the windows of Heaven and pour out His blessings.

In the simplest sense, when a person gives 10% of their income back to God, they are showing Him that they believe He will keep His word. When a person refuses to tithe, they are telling God that they do not trust Him.

"Even from the days of your fathers ye are gone away from mine ordinances, and have not kept them. Return unto me, and I will return unto you, saith the LORD of hosts. But ye said, Wherein shall we return? Will a man rob God? Yet ye have robbed me. But ye say, Wherein have we robbed thee? In tithes and offerings. Ye are cursed with a curse: for ye have robbed me, even this whole nation.

Bring ye all the tithes into the storehouse, that there may be meat in mine house, and prove me now herewith, saith the LORD of hosts, if I will not open you the windows of heaven, and pour you out a blessing, that there shall not be room enough to receive it."
Malachi 3:7-10

God challenges you to test Him in this matter of tithing and see if He will keep His promise. In fact, God begs you to test Him. When a person has enough faith in God's promise to give Him back a small percentage of what He gave them in the first place, God is very pleased. Without faith it is impossible to please Him.[5]

YOUR TITHE PREVENTS THE DESTROYER

Tithing is not amoral. Tithing is not optional. There is no middle ground. Either you are tithing, and God is blessing you; or you are not tithing, and God is cursing you.

"And I will rebuke the devourer for your sakes, and he shall not destroy the fruits of your ground; neither shall your vine cast her fruit before the time in the field, saith the LORD of hosts."
Malachi 3:11

When a person decides to trust God and give Him 10% of their income, then God begins to add to what they already have. When a person decides that God cannot meet their needs if they give up 10% of their income, then God begins to take away what He has already given them.

I find it very interesting that people who tithe are never the same people who are asking me if they can borrow money.

"Now therefore thus saith the LORD of hosts; Consider your ways. Ye have sown much, and bring in little; ye eat, but ye have not enough; ye drink, but ye are not filled with drink; ye clothe you, but there is none warm; and he that earneth wages earneth wages to put it into a bag with holes."   Haggai 1:5, 6

Ask yourself this: Why would you refuse to give God His tithe when He tells you that if you do not, He will make the 100% of your income become 90%, 80%, 50%, or even less? Wouldn't you rather give God 10% of your income and then let Him increase the remaining 90% by 10%, 20%, 50%, or even more? Tithing allows God to truly bless you.

If God was able to give you your entire income to begin with, then isn't He big enough to give you more after you have returned His share? You may not know where the additional money is going to come from, but He does. God has made a promise. He is testing your faith. Are you able to trust Him and take Him at His Word?

YOUR TITHE PLANTS THE SEED FOR MORE

There is an indisputable principle in the Bible that you get what you give. This is taught in many different places in the Word of God and is also evident in everyday life. If you want to receive a smile, give a smile. If you want to get punched, throw a punch. If you plant corn, you will harvest corn. If you give love, you will receive love. If you give money, then you will receive money.

When you trust God enough to give your tithe, then He knows He can trust you, and He will put more money under your stewardship.

"He that hath pity upon the poor lendeth unto the LORD; and that which he hath given will he pay him again."   Proverbs 19:17

"Cast thy bread upon the waters: for thou shalt find it after many days."   Ecclesiastes 11:1

YOUR TITHE KEEPS YOU GIVING

God knows that we are naturally selfish creatures, and that if we are left to ourselves we will soon become consumed with our own wants and wishes. Giving God 10% of everything we receive forces us to think outside of ourselves.

Generosity does not come naturally. It is an act that must be done by our fleshly body, but which is of the spirit and is contrary to the flesh.[6] It is an attribute for which we must be trained. Tithing is one of the steps in that training.

"He that hath a bountiful eye shall be blessed; for he giveth of his bread to the poor." Proverbs 22:9

YOUR TITHE SUPPORTS GOD'S WORK

The Israelites were commanded to give the tithe to the temple so that those working full-time for the Lord would have food to eat. In Malachi, Israel was commanded to bring all of *"...the tithes into the storehouse, that there may be meat in mine house..."*

Today, Christians are commanded to bring their tithes and offerings to their local church on Sunday in order to fund the work of God. God places in each church the people that He desires to get His work done. No church would have financial difficulties if everyone in that church tithed as they are commanded to do.

"Upon the first day of the week let every one of you lay by him in store, as God hath prospered him, that there be no gatherings when I come." 1 Corinthians 16:2

The phrase *"as God hath prospered him"* indicates a percentage. As God has blessed you, you ought to support your church. If you are not willing to support your local church, then why are you there?

When you tithe you are rewarded for being obedient, and then you are rewarded again for helping the Kingdom of God.

"Then there shall be a place which the LORD your God shall choose to cause his name to dwell there; thither shall ye bring all that I command you; your burnt offerings, and your sacrifices, your tithes, and the heave offering of your hand, and all your choice vows which ye vow unto the LORD:" Deuteronomy 12:11

One Sunday morning when I was twelve years old, my father gave me a dollar. He handed me one dime and ninety pennies. He explained to me that the ninety pennies were mine to keep, but that the dime belonged to God. He then told me that every dollar that I earned for the rest of my life was to be divided the same way. A short time later I dropped that dime in the offering plate and enjoyed the pleasure of knowing that I was being obedient both to my dad and to God.

From that day until this, I have given God ten cents out of every dollar I have ever received. God has blessed me constantly in my life. He has proven true to His promise. My life is a testimony to the truth that God blesses tithing.

If you refuse to submit to God in this area you might as well put this book down right now, because God will be unable to bless you in anything else that you do with your finances.

Will you commit to giving God 10% of everything you get?

[1] Leviticus 27:30
[2] 2 Chronicles 31:4-6, 11-12
[3] Nehemiah 13:9-12
[4] Amos 4:4; Malachi 3:8-10
[5] Hebrews 11:6
[6] Galatians 5:17

DEALING WITH DEBT

"The rich ruleth over the poor, and the borrower is servant to the lender." Proverbs 22:7

This verse sums up a lot of truth in just a few words. Nowhere in the Bible are we told that it is a sin to borrow. There are actually a few situations where it makes sense to go into debt. But don't run down to the nearest mall or department store in order to max out your credit cards just yet. There are some very important facts that you need to understand about debt.

First, you must realize that if you borrow money you will be spending much of your time working for other people. When you have debts hanging over your head, it can be frustrating to go to work knowing that a large portion of your paycheck is going to be handed over to someone else.

This means that after you have given God the tithe, and after the government has taken their share, your remaining time and energy will be used to put money into someone else's bank account. For most people this is a very difficult thing to accept. So before you sign anything that places you in another person's debt, be sure to ask yourself if you really want to be their servant for the length of time that it will take you to discharge your debt.

Second, you must understand that you will pay back more, and oftentimes MUCH more, than you originally borrowed. Anytime you borrow money, you will pay an additional fee to use that money until it is paid back. You will pay rent on that money.

The rent on borrowed money is called "interest." The Biblical term is "usury." You pay to "use" their money. In some cases, by the time a person has discharged their debt they will have paid more money in interest than the amount that they originally borrowed. In other words, when you choose to buy something with credit you may pay more than twice as much for that item.

Third, understand that you must pay it back. God has only one judgment in this matter, and He has made that judgment very clear in His Word. If you borrow money from someone and do not pay it back, you are wicked and you are a thief.

"The wicked borroweth, and payeth not again: but the righteous sheweth mercy, and giveth."   Psalm 37:21

Dear friend, bankruptcy is not an option for a Christian. Even if you went to court and had your debt legally removed, God still sees you as a debtor. Before you begin to borrow money, you should know where the money is going to come from to repay the loan. If you do not have a solid plan to repay the loan, don't borrow the money. It is that simple. Do not become a thief by defaulting on your debts.

Fourth, you must be able to pay back the full amount that you have borrowed at any time during the life of the loan. In other words, you should be able to sell whatever you have purchased with the borrowed money and recoup the entire amount that is still owed.

Here is the key question: If you borrow $500 to purchase a perishable item and have to repay the debt the next day, would you still be able to sell that item for $500 to pay back the debt? The answer is an obvious, "No!"

Any item that loses value faster than the debt can be paid should only be purchased with cash. This guideline will keep you from ever facing bankruptcy. It will also keep you from buying a bunch of junk.

Fifth, you must never go into debt for someone else. Determine right now that you will NEVER be a guarantor on another's debts. If a bank or a finance company distrusts someone's ability to repay their debts so much that they require someone else to sign for it, then why would you trust them? This is one situation that you ought to run away from as fast as you can. Our government and our financial institutions may allow such a process, but God does not.

"Be not thou one of them that strike hands, or of them that are sureties for debts. If thou hast nothing to pay, why should he take away thy bed from under thee?" Proverbs 22:26, 27

Sixth, you ought to have a goal to get completely out of debt. In this lesson you will see three examples where it could be a good idea to borrow money, but your long-term goal is still to be debt-free.

"For the LORD thy God blesseth thee, as he promised thee: and thou shalt lend unto many nations, but thou shalt not borrow; and thou shalt reign over many nations, but they shall not reign over thee."
Deuteronomy 15:6

Some have mistakenly taught that it is a sin to have any debt at all. The verse they most commonly use to propagate this teaching is found in the book of Romans.

"Owe no man any thing, but to love one another: for he that loveth another hath fulfilled the law." Romans 13:8

The command that I must owe no man anything is very clear. The confusion comes when the amount that I owe is incorrectly defined. If I go down to my local bank and borrow $1,000 with an agreement to repay $20 each month, then how much do I owe the next day? The answer is nothing. I don't owe anything yet.

How much will I owe the following month? The answer is $20. Those who would say that I owe the entire amount miss two important facts:

First, I have agreed to pay back $20 on a certain day each week, and I do not owe that money until that day arrives. This is both practical and logical.

If someone insists that I owe the whole amount, then logically I would also have to pay my electric bill, my phone bill, my rent, my taxes, and my tithe on a daily, or even on an hourly basis.

Actually, if you take this line of reasoning to the extreme I would have to pay all of these bills in advance in order to not owe anything. And if I do that then the person I just paid owes me electricity, or the use of my house, or the use of my phone, and so I have caused them to owe me.

The crucial fact here is that I do not owe anything until the day that both the lender and I have agreed upon. At that point in time the money owed becomes custom, and I become the customer. This is referred to in the verse immediately prior to the last one.

"Render therefore to all their dues: tribute to whom tribute is due; custom to whom custom; fear to whom fear; honour to whom honour." Romans 13:7

Second, the person who loaned me that money does not want it all back immediately. They want me to pay it back over time so they can earn interest. They are using my loan as a means of income, and if I pay it all back they are unable to make that money.

One of God's promised blessings to Israel was that if they obeyed His commandments, they would be in a position to lend to other nations and so earn usury. God gave His approval to this means of making money.[1] God would never give His approval to a plan that forced the other party to commit sin. If God has given me permission to be the lender, then obviously He has also given His permission for the other person to be the borrower.

THE SIX RULES OF DEBT

I should never borrow money unless...
1. I understand that I will be working for someone else.
2. I realize that I will pay back more than I borrowed.
3. I already know how I will pay it back.
4. The purchased item will always be worth more than what I owe.
5. I am willing to take full responsibility to pay off the entire loan.
6. I will eventually be completely debt-free.

Now let me give you three different situations where you might consider borrowing money. Please notice the word "consider." None of these situations are an automatic reason for borrowing. With proper planning and forethought, however, you could find that borrowing money will put you in a better situation financially.

FASTER DEBT REPAYMENT

It may be possible to borrow money at a lower interest rate in order to pay off loans that have a higher interest rate. If you have a number of smaller loans at higher interest rates, it may be possible to consolidate those loans into one larger loan at a lower interest rate. If you have a credit card debt paying 21% interest, an installment plan paying 16% interest, and a cash loan financed at 18% interest; it may make sense to take out a single loan at 7% interest and consolidate the three smaller loans.

WARNING! This plan will only get you into deeper trouble unless you determine that you will never borrow money again without following the six rules of debt. This is not meant to be an ongoing procedure. This is a one-time fix intended to help someone who has mismanaged their finances to get out of trouble more quickly.

Some people have consolidated all of their smaller loans into one big loan, only to realize that their credit cards can now be used again. The credit cards are again maxed out, new loans are signed, and they quickly find themselves in a worse situation than they were before. If you decide to use this plan, then get out a pair of scissors and cut up your credit cards. No more installment plans. No more borrowing from the family. No more quick cash loans. Sit down with your spouse and make a solemn vow to follow the six rules of debt.

You must also make sure that the payments on your new loan equal the combined total payments of all of your previous loans. If you give in to the temptation of a new lower minimum payment, you will be in debt for a very long time.

In 2 Kings 4, a young widow was left with a crushing amount of debt when her husband died. This passage is sometimes used to show that debt is bad, and in this case the debt was bad because the young widow had nothing to sell to repay the debts.

Creditors were knocking at her door and threatening to enslave her two sons to pay her bills. The widow went to the man of God for financial advice. You will notice that Elisha's advice to the widow was to borrow in order to get out of her financial troubles.

"Then he said, Go, borrow thee vessels abroad of all thy neighbours, even empty vessels; borrow not a few."   2 Kings 4:3

Elisha told her to borrow, and to borrow big, in order to get out of debt. Certainly God miraculously intervened in this case, but it is also clear that this lady got herself out of financial difficulty by borrowing. This idea may seem like you are going backwards, but if a "better" debt can be used to pay off a "worse" debt, you will probably be better off. Be sure to seek Godly counsel before following this plan.

BUYING YOUR OWN HOME

It is a fact of life that everyone must live somewhere. In some situations it is actually cheaper to pay for a mortgage, taxes, and insurance for your own home than it would be to rent a comparable house. If this is the case, it is often wiser to own the house and allow your equity in it to grow. Your equity is the part that you own.

After ten years, you will own a large portion of your home – maybe thousands of dollars' worth. If you were to rent for that same ten years, at the end all you would have is a pile of rent receipts, and only then if you can remember where you stored them!

If you take out a loan to purchase a home, it is possible that after making payments for ten years you will find that your house is worth more than when you started.

You may even find that the equity caused by growth is greater than the equity gained by making regular payments. There are very few other purchases where this is a possibility.

It is rarely a good idea to buy a home unless you are going to live there for a minimum of three years. If you move sooner than that, agent fees and legal fees will eat up your equity.

Again, there is no blanket answer for everyone. Every situation is different, and you will need to get good advice from a competent financial advisor. It is also very important that your home purchase still meets the six rules of debt.

HIGH RETURN INVESTMENTS

As you increase in financial wisdom, you may come across an investment that pays a very good return for which you do not have the available funds. It may be wise to borrow money at a lower interest rate in order to buy into an investment that pays a higher interest rate.

One example would be a rental property that has a net return of 12%. If you can find a mortgage for 5%, then you would come out ahead by borrowing.

This is a complicated area and should not be entered into without considerable knowledge and expert advice. The uninformed can find themselves in serious financial trouble by investing without fully understanding the risks.

There may be other situations where borrowing money makes good sense, but these are usually in specialized situations that are beyond the scope of this book.

Now suppose you have the opportunity to take out a loan at 8% interest. Which of these things would you even consider using the loan to buy?

New stereo	Groceries
Second-hand car	Investment with a 9% return
New living room set	Cigarettes
Music CDs	Financial books
Tools	Helping out a friend
University education	Investment with a 25% return
Electric bill	Family home
Your tithe	Credit card with 21% interest
Faith Promise Missions	Lottery tickets
Clothes	Loan from a family member
Christmas presents	Television
Home renovations	Pay off a cash loan at 18% interest

Allow me to take a couple of pages and talk you through some of these individual examples to help you see how the rules of debt should be applied to each one.

Wouldn't it be great to own a brand new stereo with all of the latest technology? Of course it would. But before you lay down your credit card and add another $159.99 plus tax to the balance, let me ask you a question. How much will that stereo be worth once you walk out the door?

If you took that stereo directly to a pawn shop, you might be offered $50. Selling it on an online auction might get you a little more, but still nowhere near what you paid for it. In other words, within seconds of buying it you are holding an item that is worth half of what you owe. This violates the fourth law of debt.

This same principle also applies to buying groceries, a new living room set, music CDs, clothes, Christmas presents, or a television. It is especially true of lottery tickets and cigarettes, both of which would be wrong to buy anyway.

Lottery tickets are basically a government tax on stupidity, and smoking cigarettes is just slowly committing suicide while watching your money go up in smoke.

If you are borrowing money to pay for things like your tithe, Faith Promise Missions, or your electric bill, you have a serious problem with priorities. You should be paying these through your new budget.

Paying for a university education, financial books, or tools may allow you to make more money, but none of them should be purchased with credit. They may feel like a necessity, but they cannot be sold for enough money to pay back your debt. You should wait until you can pay cash.

A second-hand car may help you to work a second job and earn more income. Always remember that you should only borrow money for a vehicle when you are able to make a down payment large enough that if you were forced to sell the car, you could immediately repay the loan in full.

Taking out a loan to renovate your house may improve your living conditions and raise the value of your home on paper, but if something goes wrong and you have to repay the debt quickly you would have to sell your home. Once again it is better to wait until you have the cash.

Borrowing money at 8% so you can invest it at 9% is a fool's game. Even if the investment is a success, by the time that you pay taxes on your profits you will lose money.

Borrowing money at 8% so that you can invest it at 25% may make sense. Keep in mind that investments with returns like this are rarely available and are often a farce. Tread carefully. When you are offered a return like this you are almost always getting paid to take on a huge risk.

It may be wise to borrow money to pay off a credit card with 21% interest or a cash loan with 18% interest, but only if you have the character to avoid borrowing any more money or using the credit cards again.

Buying your home is usually only possible with a mortgage. Only do so after reviewing the six laws of debt, and after making sure that you will be living there for a minimum of three years. Again, your down payment should be large enough that you could sell the house for enough money to pay off the remaining part of the mortgage.

Borrowing money to help out a friend or pay back a loan from a family member may make you feel better initially, but it may make you feel terrible later. Sharing this book with your friends and family may help them to understand why you must say no.

[1] Deuteronomy 23:20

ELIMINATING DEBT

"Let all things be done decently and in order." 1 Corinthians 14:40

In this chapter you are going to learn a simple system which will help you eliminate all of your debts. Before going further, be sure that you have carefully read and understood Chapters 7 and 10.

In Chapter 7 you were directed to make a list of all of your debts. This list includes everything you owe that you will one day no longer have to pay. Your goal is to eventually eliminate everything on this list.

For each of your debts, you will need to know three numbers: the amount you owe, the minimum payment, and the interest rate. Using these three numbers you are going to prioritize your debts so that you can pay them off as quickly as possible. Write these three numbers next to the company or individual to whom the money is owed. Your completed list may look something like this:

Lender	Total Debt	Minimum	Interest Rate
Home Mortgage	$80,000	$515	7%
Bank of America Visa	1,500	30	18%
Chase Freedom Card	2,000	38	16%
Car Payment	8,500	225	12%
Checking Overdraft	300	12	16%
JC Penney Credit Card	650	50	27%

Now, rearrange these bills so that the interest rates ascend from lowest to highest. If two debts have the same interest rate, list the one with the largest minimum payment first.

In this list, your home mortgage would be removed since you still have more than five years of payments. If you want to pay off your home mortgage early, you should do so only after all of your other debts have been paid. Until then, consider your monthly mortgage payment as one of your bills. Your new list will look like this:

Lender	Total Debt	Minimum	Interest Rate
JC Penney Credit Card	$ 650	50	27%
Bank of America Visa	1,500	30	18%
Chase Freedom Card	2,000	38	16%
Checking Overdraft	300	12	16%
Car Payment	8,500	225	12%

Your total minimum payments each month now equal $355 per month. Your next step is to determine what percent of your monthly income that $355 represents.

If your income is less than $1,775, then your total minimum payments equal more than 20% of your monthly income. In that case you will simply make the minimum payments until your debts total less than 20% of your monthly income.

At this point, the crucial thing is to stop adding to your debts. You should not finance a new car. You should not use your credit card or borrow more money. If you keep adding to your debts you will never achieve your goal. Initially you will tithe, pay off your debts, pay your bills, and live off the rest.

If your monthly income is between $1,775 and $3,550, you have a choice. You should still use at least 10% of your income to pay off your debts, and you can use as much as 20%.

If, however, the total of your minimum payments is less than 20%, you may choose to begin putting the difference into savings. You will learn how to do that in Chapter 12.

If your monthly income is more than $3,550 you will still use 10% of your income to pay off your debts. You will make the minimum payment for all of the debts on your list, starting at the top and working down the list.

When you finally have only one debt left on your list, you will put everything that you have left of the 10% toward that debt.

Example: If you make $4,000 per month, you would tithe 10% or $400, use 10% or $400 to pay your debts, and put 10% or $400 into savings. You would then use the remaining amount to pay your bills and live off the rest. When applying this concept to your income, always remember that percentages are the most important thing.

Of the $400 that you put toward paying off your debts, you would use $225 for your car payment, $38 for your Chase Freedom Card, $12 for your checking overdraft, and $30 for your Bank of America Visa. You would then take the remaining $95 and pay it ALL on your JC Penney Credit Card.

After doing this for seven months, you will have completely paid off your JC Penney Credit Card. The next month you would use $225 for your car payment, $38 for your Chase Freedom Card, $12 for your checking overdraft, and you would take the remaining $125 and pay it all on your Bank of America Visa. In another six months you would completely pay off your Bank of America Visa. Continue in this way until you have eliminated all of your debts.

Everyone's situation is different, and this plan is not set in stone. You need to find what works for you. The important thing is to decide what you are going to do, and then stick with your plan until your debts are all paid.

Here are three ways that you could adjust the plan to fit your particular situation:

TEN PERCENT OF WHAT?

Remember that God commands that you tithe on your income. This is never optional. When God demands His 10%, He means your first 10%. That means that you should tithe on your gross income. You are giving God His tithe before the government takes their portion.

"Honour the LORD with thy substance, and with the firstfruits of all thine increase:"   Proverbs 3:9

When determining the amount you will use for paying your debts and saving, however, you may decide to use a figure that is 10% of your net income. Your net income is what you have after the government has taken out your taxes.

Example: If you are single and make $4,000 per month, you will pay approximately $1,000 per month for taxes. You would still need to pay your tithe on your gross income, but you could figure your 10% for debt payments and savings from your net income of $3,000. This means that you would pay $400 for your tithe, $300 toward your debts, and $300 into savings. You would then pay your bills and live from the remaining $2,000.

PAYING OFF YOUR MORTGAGE

A second option is available if you have a mortgage. You may want to include your home mortgage in your list of debts even if you have more than five years left to pay. Of course, doing so will mean that you have less money to pay on your higher interest debts.

If adding your mortgage payment to your list of debts takes your minimum payments over 20% of your income, it will also mean that it will take longer before you have money to put into savings. This option may be discouraging in the long term and needs to be carefully considered before being implemented.

Normally my recommendation is to pay all your other debts first, while keeping your mortgage in the bills category. Once all of your other debts are eliminated, you could then use the entire 10% designated for debts to pay off your mortgage.

NO MINIMUM PAYMENT AND NO INTEREST

There have been many times when I have helped someone put together a list of their debts, only to find that some of those debts have no minimum payments or interest. Usually this is money that has been borrowed from friends or family members.

Using the plan given in this chapter, these loans would end up at the bottom of the list and they would be paid last. There is, however, another aspect to these loans that must be taken into consideration. When you owe money to a finance company or a credit card company, they won't be coming to your family reunion. Spending time with a friend or family member to whom you owe money can be a very uncomfortable situation.

If owing money to a friend or relative is causing a rift in your relationship, it may be wise to put the numbers aside for a few months and pay your friend or family back first. Sometimes the math doesn't work, but it is better to have them smiling at you again. Use your own discretion!

SAVING FOR WINTER

"There is treasure to be desired and oil in the dwelling of the wise; but a foolish man spendeth it up."   Proverbs 21:20

How much money will you make in your lifetime? If you make $25,000 a year (an average wage in America) and you work for 40 years (from 25 years old to 65 years old) you will have earned approximately $1,000,000 over the course of your working life. If you continue to be average, you will have almost none of that $1,000,000 left when you retire.

The purpose of this lesson is to implant this one thought permanently into your mind:

What matters is not how much money you make, but how much you keep and what you do with it.

America is a wonderful country with many freedoms available to its citizens. According to the averages, however, less than 5% of Americans are self-supporting by the time they retire at age 65. Of the other 95%, about one-third have died, and the rest are dependent in some way upon the government.

America has a history of taking care of its own citizens. When Social Security was begun in 1935, there were about 160 workers paying into the Social Security program for every one person receiving benefits. Within ten years there were only four workers for every one person receiving benefits. In recent years the number of workers to beneficiaries has dropped to less than three. This is obviously unsustainable.

There will come a day when Social Security will no longer be able to support itself. On at least twelve different occasions Social Security has had to borrow from other sources in order to pay out benefits. God never places the responsibility for your future support on your government. He places all of the responsibility squarely on you!

The only two options that your government has to correct this situation is to increase taxes or to reduce benefits, both of which they have been doing for some time. Many thousands of people are feeling the squeeze as their cost of living increases while their benefit checks remain the same. There has even been talk of Social Security benefits being taxed.

If this frightens you a little, it should. Too many Christians go through life with their head in the sand, assuming that when they reach retirement age the government will care for them as it did for their parents and grandparents.

The wisest preacher in the Old Testament, King Solomon, commanded us to go to a tiny teacher that has this whole concept down to a fine art. We are told in Proverbs to go to the ant.

"Go to the ant, thou sluggard; consider her ways, and be wise; Which having no guide, overseer, or ruler, provideth her meat in the summer, and gathereth her food in the harvest. How long wilt thou sleep, O sluggard? When wilt thou arise out of thy sleep? Yet a little sleep, a little slumber, a little folding of the hands to sleep: So shall thy poverty come as one that travelleth, and thy want as an armed man." Proverbs 6:6-11

The Bible compares our life to the cycle of seasons. Spring represents our childhood. Summer pictures the young adult years. Harvest is middle age. Winter is the retirement years. The ant uses her summer and harvest months to get ready for winter.

Here we see an illustration of one who plans in his early years for the latter part of his life. God has made this little insect wise enough to know that things will not always be as they are now, so preparation must be made for how things will be then.

You may be working now, but there will come a day when you can no longer work. You may be earning good money today, but how long would you survive if that flow of income suddenly stopped?

Before you stick your head back in the sand, perhaps you should visit a nursing home and speak to some of the residents there. It may shock you to learn how many have spent everything they had and are now totally dependent on the good graces of government funding.

If you are living on an income provided by a government benefit, perhaps you should ask yourself what would happen if that benefit were cut in half. Governments do change. Government policies also change. Although the government does try to take care of its people, there are limits to what they can do.

According to God's Word, it is not up to the government to provide you an income for all of your living years. That is up to you. It is not up to the government to care for your family after you are gone. That is also up to you.

"But if any provide not for his own, and specially for those of his own house, he hath denied the faith, and is worse than an infidel."
1 Timothy 5:8

In order to care for you and your family in future years, you must arrange to have a steady stream of income that does not require you to work. Your money must be saved and then invested in order to bring in an income. You could say it this way:

***I am working to earn my money so that one day
my money will work for me.***

This money will come from your savings. Those people who claim that they cannot save are really saying that they refuse to think about the future. The 10% to 20% of your income that you save now will provide you with income when you reach your winter years.

You are now about to learn the BIG SECRET to saving. Are you ready? Don't miss this! It will make a huge difference later in life.

Get your money into a savings account before you see it.

If you are like most people, you spend whatever you have. If you have $10, you will spend it. If you have a $100, you will spend it. If someone handed you a $1000, you would spend it. The money comes in and the money goes out, and there is never any left. This is why people think that they cannot save. They say, "I have been trying to save for years, and there is never any left."

Take out your tithe, pay your debts, put 10% into savings, and then go ahead and spend the rest. You will find that all of your money is still gone by the end of the month, but your savings account will be growing. In the next chapter we will discuss investing the money you have saved, but that lesson will not help you if you have not begun to save.

Here are some hints to help you get started:

1. Open a separate savings account.
2. Get a high interest account that penalizes early withdrawals.
3. Create an automatic transfer into savings on your payday.
4. Don't touch the money in that account.
5. Start saving something immediately. (Saving is a habit!)
6. As you pay off your debts, increase your savings to 20%.

WISE INVESTING

"The rich man's wealth is his strong city: the destruction of the poor is their poverty."　　　　　　　　　　　　　　　　Proverbs 10:15

"For the kingdom of heaven is as a man travelling into a far country, who called his own servants, and delivered unto them his goods. And unto one he gave five talents, to another two, and to another one; to every man according to his several ability; and straightway took his journey. Then he that had received the five talents went and traded with the same, and made them other five talents. And likewise he that had received two, he also gained other two. But he that had received one went and digged in the earth, and hid his lord's money. After a long time the lord of those servants cometh, and reckoneth with them. And so he that had received five talents came and brought other five talents, saying, Lord, thou deliverest unto me five talents: behold, I have gained beside them five talents more. His lord said unto him, Well done, thou good and faithful servant: thou hast been faithful over a few things, I will make thee ruler over many things: enter thou into the joy of thy lord. He also that had received two talents came and said, Lord, thou deliveredst unto me two talents: behold, I have gained two other talents beside them. His lord said unto him, Well done, good and faithful servant; thou hast been faithful over a few things, I will make thee ruler over many things: enter thou into the joy of thy lord. Then he which had received the one talent came and said, Lord, I knew thee that thou art an hard man, reaping where thou has not sown, and gathering where thou hast not strawed: And I was afraid, and went and hid thy talent in the earth: lo, there thou hast that is thine. His lord answered and said unto him, Thou wicked and slothful servant, thou knewest that I reap where I sowed not, and gather where I have not strawed: Thou oughtest therefore to have put my money to the exchangers, and then at my coming I should have received mine own with usury. Take therefore the talent from him, and give it unto him which hath ten talents."　　　　　　　　　　　Matthew 25:14-28

This is a story that Jesus used as an illustration during His preaching. Although the main purpose of Jesus' sermon was not investing, He certainly put His stamp of approval on it. For now we will lay aside the doctrines of Jesus' teaching and focus on the story itself.

The talent was a Biblical measurement of money. It could have been either gold or silver. Did you notice that the two servants who invested the money that had been entrusted to them were commended and rewarded, while the lazy servant who did not invest was condemned and punished?

Investing simply means using money in order to make more money. The result may be either a lump sum or regular flow of income. These returns are then reinvested to earn even more money.

You may have also noticed that two types of investing were mentioned in this parable. The first two servants chose to invest by trading. This means they used their knowledge to purchase something and then to resell it at a higher price. By using the first method of *active investing*, they gained the praise of their master.

After condemning the lazy servant for his lack of action, the master suggested that he could have at least used *passive investing* by giving the money to someone else and letting them make a profit. The master would have then received interest. Although Jesus did not give the specifics of these men's investing procedures, we can make some clear conclusions from the facts that God has given us in this parable:

THE MEN HAD DIFFERING ABILITIES

We learn here that the master gave each man a different amount depending on their abilities. Then they invested according to their abilities. The man with the greatest ability was able to take five talents and turn them into ten. The man with two talents was able to turn them into four. The man with no ability could have put the money in the bank and earned interest, but he was too lazy.

The first two men were not commended because of how much ability they had, but because they used the ability that they had. Through using the abilities that they had, their abilities increased and they were then given greater opportunities.

THE TWO WHO TRIED SUCCEEDED

It may be that they failed initially and maybe even that they failed more than once. However "after a long time" they doubled their money. A mistake in this area is not failure. Failure is one of the steps to success. The mistake is in not trying. If you shoot at nothing you will hit it every time.

THE TWO SUCCESSFUL MEN MADE THE EFFORT

Many people who have money to invest desire to make good returns, but they do not want to take the time to learn about investing. They convince themselves that this area is too difficult to understand, and as a result they lose some or all of their potential gains. Many people put investing into the "too hard" basket and never get it done.

THE LAZY MAN HAD MANY EXCUSES

The first two servants had the same excuses, and they still went out and got tremendous results. No matter what method you decide to use for investing, someone is bound to come along and tell you horror stories about someone who lost everything doing the same thing. Never let others' mistakes paralyze you with fear. The lazy man's master scolded him because he wouldn't even put the money in the bank and earn interest. Through fear of loss, he refused to even try.

The lazy man's money went to the man that understood investing. We see the same principle at work in society today. Despite all of the government's best efforts, the rich keep getting richer and the poor keep getting poorer. Money always flows toward knowledge.

> *"Riches and honour are with me; yea, durable riches and righteousness. My fruit is better than gold, yea, than fine gold; and my revenue than choice silver. I lead in the way of righteousness, in the midst of the paths of judgment: That I may cause those that love me to inherit substance; and I will fill their treasures."*
>
> Wisdom speaking in Proverbs 8:18-21

Having seen that the principle of investing is a Biblical principle, we are now going to look at the practical side of investing. The following principles are very important for the successful investor. Before going any further, it is imperative that you have already implemented the budget given in Chapter 8.

Trying to invest before you have your financial house in order is like trying to put a roof on before you have laid the foundation. Don't fall into the trap of trying to earn high returns when you are still struggling to buy groceries.

DO WHAT YOU KNOW

I have counseled many people on finances, and there have been numerous times when someone has asked a question something like this: "I have $1,000. What should I invest in?" This is a difficult question to answer because the person asking this question should probably not invest in the same things I do.

Investing is a very personal thing, and what works for one person may not work for someone else. I would suggest that anyone ready to begin investing should invest only in what they know, what they understand, and what they enjoy. If you cannot get excited about a particular investment, it is probably not for you.

Successful investing is a long-term proposition, and if you get into something that you will tire of quickly, you may decide to pull out of it at a time that is disadvantageous for you. This is not to say that your heart has to flutter when you look at your investment account, but you do have to be willing to stay with it.

KNOW WHAT YOUR GOALS ARE

Are you trying to make a quick return, or are you trying to set up a long-term income stream? How much risk can you handle? How long will it be before you need your money back? The answers to these questions will help you to determine what types of investments are best for you.

GET HELP

One way to guarantee failure is to try to do everything yourself. Investing is a team effort. You need to surround yourself with a good team of advisors and counselors, always remembering that you are the captain of the team.

Having a dependable lawyer, accountant, tax advisor, mortgage broker, stockbroker, real estate agent, tradesman, or contractor can make all the difference. Please make sure that these people really do know what they are doing. Nothing is more expensive than free advice from someone who has never actually done it.

"Where no counsel is, the people fall: but in the multitude of counsellors there is safety." Proverbs 11:14

"The way of a fool is right in his own eyes: but he that hearkeneth unto counsel is wise." Proverbs 12:15

DECIDE ON YOUR INPUT

All investing takes time, but some methods of investing take much more time than others. The time required does not necessarily equate to the rate of return.

You may find an investment that offers a 3% return and takes five minutes per month, or you may find an investment that offers a 5% return and takes thirty hours per month. Be sure your investments will not demand more of your time than you want to give.

BE PATIENT

Every investment offers windows of time that will give you the opportunity to greatly increase your return. Those who understand their investments get in while the prices are low, and get out when the prices are high. Those who are trusting their luck or their emotions get in when the prices are high and get out when the prices are low, thus creating another horror story to scare potential investors. Don't be afraid to go against the crowd when you know what you are doing. Don't try to get rich quick.

"Cast thy bread upon the waters: for thou shalt find it after many days."   Ecclesiastes 11:1

IDEAS FOR ACTIVE AND PASSIVE INVESTING
Online auctions
Physical auctions
Estate auctions
Annuities
Savings accounts
Certificates of deposit
Bank investment funds
Commercial leases
Commodities trading
Currency trading
Equipment leases
Franchise fees
Futures contracts
Hedge funds
Automobile insurance
Health insurance
Life insurance
Property insurance
Lease purchases
Lease options
Letters of credit
Mutual funds

Automobile notes
Business notes
Collectibles notes
Equipment notes
Mortgage notes
Partnership agreements
Real estate capital appreciation
Real estate cash flow
Real estate flipping
Real estate mortgagee auctions
Real estate options
Commercial real estate
Industrial real estate
Residential real estate
Royalties
Stock dividends
Stock market index funds
Stock options
Short selling stocks
Trading stocks
Tax liens
Tax refunds
Time share memberships
Trust advances

Many of these investments can be combined or will overlap. This is by no means an exhaustive list. This list is just to give you an idea of the many options available. New methods of investing are constantly being created. Any situation where money is given with the purpose of regaining it with increase can be considered an investment.

You can always invest in a simpler method while you are in the process of learning a more complicated method. Your goal is to wisely use your Lord's money to make more money.

LAYING UP TREASURES

"Lay not up for yourselves treasures upon earth, where moth and rust doth corrupt, and where thieves break through and steal: But lay up for yourselves treasures in heaven, where neither moth nor rust doth corrupt, and where thieves do not break through nor steal: For where your treasure is, there will your heart be also."
Matthew 6:19-21

The word "treasure" is found, in its different forms, ninety-seven times in the King James Bible. The Bible is very positive about investing, but it takes an entirely different view about laying up treasures. The Bible commands us to not lay up treasures on earth. The Bible tells us that we should lay up treasures in Heaven.

What exactly are treasures? Treasures are items of stored value.

Everything that you own falls into one of three broad categories. Some of the things that you own are used regularly, and to lose them would cause inconvenience. These may be things you use every day, or they may be things you use once every six months.

Possessions that fall into this category are called **GOODS**. This category would include things like your house, car, bedding, dishes, tools, appliances, computers, food, and toys. The word "goods" is used forty-two times in the Bible, and in every case it refers to belongings or property that are necessary or important for living.

Some things that you own bring you an income. They may bring in money by the way they are used, or they may bring in money of their own accord. Possessions in this category are labeled as **ASSETS** or **INVESTMENTS**. These are things that you own because of the money that they provide for you.

Some possessions do not fit into either of these categories. They are not used regularly, and sometimes not at all. They bring in no income and produce nothing of value.

These possessions are things that you keep because they have some value to you or because you hope that someday they will have value to someone else. These possessions are called **TREASURES**.

"Sell that ye have, and give alms; provide yourselves bags which wax not old, a treasure in the heavens that faileth not, where no thief approacheth, neither moth corrupteth. For where your treasure is, there will your heart be also." Luke 12:33, 34

When the Lord commanded us to sell what we have and to invest it in Heaven, He did not intend that we take the food off our children's plates and sell it to put money in the offering plates. His intention was not that we sell all of our clothes or put our houses on the market in order to support missionaries. Our God is a very practical God, and although He does not want us to worry about these things, He does not expect us to go without them either.

The Lord is not opposed to us making wise investments. It is an indisputable fact that those Christians who have larger incomes can give, and often do give, more than those who are poor. Be careful that you never confuse financial incompetence with spirituality.

"And Joses, who by the apostles was surnamed Barnabas, (which is, being interpreted, The son of consolation,) a Levite, and of the country of Cyprus, Having land, sold it, and brought the money, and laid it at the apostles' feet." Acts 4:36, 37

Barnabas had made some wise investments, so when some needs arose in his local church he was in a position to be of help. He sold a piece of land and donated the proceeds to the church, allowing the apostles to decide where it was needed the most.

In the previous chapter we studied Jesus' parable about a master who gave talents to three of his servants before going on a journey. Upon his return, we saw that the master commended his two servants who had wisely invested the talents that were placed in their care. They took their money and used it for investing.

The same master condemned the slothful servant who took his talent and buried it in the earth. This servant had taken his talent and turned it into an earthly treasure – or stored value.

HOW DOES THIS APPLY TO ME?

When your Master returns, you will also have to answer for whether the things given to you by Him were used as goods or investments or wasted as treasures. How many things do you have lying around your house that you are not using regularly and bring you no income? They cannot be classified as goods because they have no practical use, and they cannot be classified as investments because they are returning no income. They are treasures, and they could be converted to a much better use. Treasures carry with them four major difficulties:

THEY OFTEN LOSE VALUE

Treasures that are bought with the intention of selling them later at a higher price may lose value due to inflation. There may be considerable costs involved with purchasing and selling them, which makes it difficult for you to recoup the original cost.

Things continually fall out of fashion, and it may be that when you are ready to sell, you find that they have become an unwanted commodity. (Remember the "Beanie Baby" fad? Some people paid hundreds of dollars for these dolls, only to find later that no one wanted them.) Buying something while hoping the next person will pay more than you did is sometimes called the "greater fool theory."

THEY ARE DIFFICULT TO MAINTAIN

Many items that fall into the category of treasures are highly perishable, and there can be large costs involved in protecting them from mold, rust, moths, moisture, rot, and theft. Many times the cost of storage makes these treasures expensive to keep.

THEY CAN STEAL YOUR HEART

We rarely fall in love with our everyday possessions, and you will seldom find an investor who is in love with their investments. Treasures, however, can be very seductive, and we often fall in love with them. Few people are in love with the car they drive every day, but they give their heart to that special vehicle in the back shed that they seldom drive. Few ladies are in love with their everyday dishes, but they may be in love with the expensive china they are afraid to take out of the drawer.

THEY NEVER FULLY SATISFY

Once your heart is set on a treasure, it will never satisfy your heart. You may find your home full of treasures that once stole your heart but have since lost their appeal.

"Hell and destruction are never full; so the eyes of man are never satisfied." Proverbs 27:20

Your treasures can be sold, and the money can be used to buy either goods or investments. Some of the money should be used for the Kingdom of God so that you are placing your treasures in Heaven. There they will never lose value, they will never deteriorate, and they will keep your heart focused on the next world instead of this one.

Go through your closets and your sheds. Climb up into your attic. Find those things that you do not use and that do not bring an income. Hold a garage sale. Put an advertisement in the paper. The wealthier you are, the more likely it is that you have treasures in your house that could be converted into eternal value.

THE VERY BEST THING

"And now, brethren, I commend you to God, and to the word of his grace, which is able to build you up, and to give you an inheritance among all them which are sanctified. I have coveted no man's silver, or gold, or apparel. Yea, ye yourselves know, that these hands have ministered unto my necessities, and to them that were with me. I have shewed you all things, how that so labouring ye ought to support the weak, and to remember the words of the Lord Jesus, how he said, It is more blessed to give than to receive."

Acts 20:32-35

You and I live in an extremely selfish world. A great majority of people, both saved and unsaved, live only to please and satisfy themselves. As a result, the majority of people view money only as a means of bringing themselves more pleasure and satisfaction. Because we are surrounded by this kind of thinking every day, it is easy to assume that someone who is trying to earn or save more money must be doing it for selfish reasons.

In this passage from Acts, Paul was talking to a group of Christians at Ephesus. He made a number of interesting points in his closing words. He reminded the Ephesian brethren that he did not covet any of their gold, silver, or nice clothes. He reminded them that he worked for his own money. He reminded them that he used the money that he earned in order to meet his own needs as well as taking care of the needs of others. He then reminded them that they also ought to use the money that they earned from their work to help those who are weak. Finally, he reminds them that it is more blessed (it brings more happiness and satisfaction) to give than it does to receive.

There is a sort of pseudo-spirituality that teaches it is wrong to have money. Those who think this way feel that if someone desires to have money, they must want that money to satisfy their own desires. Since seeking one's own satisfaction is selfishness, they feel that to desire money means that someone is selfish.

In ascribing these motives to everyone, these pseudo-spiritual ones actually expose their own hearts. Accusing someone of acting with the wrong motives only displays the motives that the accuser would have if they behaved in the same manner.

"Therefore thou art inexcusable, O man, whosoever thou art that judgest: for wherein thou judgest another, thou condemnest thyself; for thou that judgest doest the same things." Romans 2:1

Sadly, in trying to prove their spirituality by not having money, these people miss the opportunity to be a blessing to others. If I only want to get money in order to satisfy myself, then I am selfish. If I want to gain money in order to help others who are in need, then I have found God's true blessing. In order to meet the needs of others, I must have money. If I claim to be spiritual because I have no money then who am I helping? In truth, that may be the ultimate selfishness.

To understand this lesson, you must understand that God's plan for gaining satisfaction is to stop seeking it for yourself and begin seeking it for others. Notice that the Apostle Paul did not want the gold, silver, and clothing that belonged to others. Paul knew that if he were to take away other people's belongings, he would not receive any satisfaction from them. Instead, Paul worked hard to earn his own money and then gave it away. As a mature Christian, the Apostle Paul knew that it was a good thing for him to have an abundance of money because he was not busy seeking his own pleasure. He was using the money to meet the needs of others. This is where the real blessing is.

Money is not wrong. Money is not evil.

The love of money is the root of all evil.

The love of money is loving money because of what it does for me.

Using money to help others brings true satisfaction.

Let's go back and look at Acts 20:32-35 again. Notice how Paul listed his priorities:

1. **I do not try to get what others have.** "*I have coveted no man's silver, or gold, or apparel.*" True satisfaction does not come from collecting the things that other people have.

2. **I take care of my necessities first.** If I get so spiritual that I do not take care of myself, then soon I will no longer be able to help anyone. It is important that I feed, clothe, and care for myself in order to keep my own ministry viable.

This principle is illustrated whenever someone flies in a commercial airplane. The air hostess explains that if cabin pressure is lost, an oxygen mask will fall from the ceiling. This mask is to be quickly fitted to your face in order for you to breathe the oxygen. The hostess then adds that if you have a child seated next to you, you should fit your own mask first. The obvious implication is that you can be of no use to that child if you are unconscious. In the same manner, if I give money away to the point where I am unclothed or starving to death, I have effectively ended my ministry to other people.

3. **I take care of those who are dependent on me.** A husband is to care for his wife. A parent is to care for their child, and later, the child is to care for their parent. In Paul's case, he took the responsibility of caring for his traveling companions.

4. **I then support those who are weak.** I give to those who are struggling. I support ministries that help people physically, mentally, emotionally, and spiritually. I use my money to lift others up and make their lives better.

5. **I am more blessed by giving than by getting.** My true satisfaction comes when I am able to give someone what he or she needs. As I mature spiritually, I will see that I receive a much bigger blessing by giving away than by getting.

"He that hath pity upon the poor lendeth unto the LORD; and that which he hath given will he pay him again." Proverbs 19:17

When I give money away, I am actually lending it to the Lord. Since the Lord always pays His debts, I will eventually get that money back. Therefore, I will have received the blessing and satisfaction of helping someone, only to be given the opportunity to do it over and over and over again.

"The desire of the slothful killeth him; for his hands refuse to labour. He coveteth greedily all the day long: but the righteous giveth and spareth not." Proverbs 21:25, 26

The slothful man is dying because he can never get enough of what he wants while the righteous man is flourishing because he is giving things away every chance he gets.

"He that hath a bountiful eye shall be blessed; for he giveth of his bread to the poor." Proverbs 22:9

A bountiful eye is not the same as a bountiful wallet. A bountiful wallet has the ability to give. A bountiful eye is looking for an opportunity to give. The Christian with a bountiful eye has found the secret of true satisfaction.

"If thine enemy be hungry, give him bread to eat; and if he be thirsty, give him water to drink: For thou shalt heap coals of fire upon his head, and the LORD shall reward thee." Proverbs 25:21, 22

The joy of giving is not dependent on the recipient. I can even choose to give to someone who hates me, and even if they criticize me, God will still bless me for giving.

God has a severe shortage of people who are living to meet the needs of others. When one of God's children decides to take Him at His Word and to bring satisfaction to other people, then God takes it upon Himself to be responsible for meeting the giver's needs.

When I give to a poor person, I have just guaranteed that I will not go without! I have just found real blessings and satisfaction. The best thing about having money is being able to give it away whenever God brings a need to your attention!

A Long Term Goal

In the beginning of my search for God's will concerning my finances, I read literally hundreds of books written by the many experts of today's financial world. These successful secular counsellors often taught one or more of the principles that I had already found in the Bible. I learned that God's truth works for anyone who applies it, whether they are a Christian or not.

As I finished book after book, however, I was left with an incomplete feeling. It was as though I had been given only half of a recipe. Each author gave more good advice from yet another angle, but their plan for my finances always seemed to fade out when they reached the point where I would die. This bothered me. Then one day, after reading through the book of Genesis once again, and after meditating upon what I had read, something clicked:

God's plan for my finances is a multi-generational plan.

If I handle my finances according to God's plan, I will not only be a blessing to my family and to others while I live on this earth, but I can continue to be a blessing to others long after I am gone.

"A good man leaveth an inheritance to his children's children: and the wealth of the sinner is laid up for the just."   Proverbs 13:22

The above verse addresses a minimum of three generations. If you are a parent, God's Word teaches that you have a two-fold responsibility: You have been tasked with leaving an inheritance for your children, and you are responsible for training them so that they know what to do with it. They can then be an even greater blessing to their children and the people they meet that are in need.

Years ago someone printed a bumper sticker which proclaimed, "We're spending our children's inheritance!" Although this was probably meant as a light-hearted jest, this type of thinking is against all that God intended for His people.

The mentality behind the phrase is as selfish as the devil. Your life is not about you, and your money is not your own. God's intention is that you carefully steward what He has given you, and that you then pass it along to the next generation which has been carefully prepared to continue that stewardship.

In the record of Abraham's life we read, *"And Abraham gave all that he had unto Isaac."*[1] Abraham certainly was not spending Isaac's inheritance. All that God gave Abraham throughout his life was carefully handled so that he could one day turn it over to his son.

A little later we read this: *"Then Isaac sowed in that land, and received in the same year an hundredfold: and the LORD blessed him. And the man waxed great, and went forward, and grew until he became very great: For he had possession of flocks, and possession of herds, and great store of servants: and the Philistines envied him."*[2]

Not only had Abraham prepared an inheritance for his son, but he had also prepared his son for the inheritance. In the Bible, the inheritance given to a child by their parent is sometimes called the birthright. The transfer of the authority to manage that inheritance is sometimes called the blessing.

This is seen clearly in two separate stories about Jacob and Esau. In the first story Esau came in hungry from hunting. In a moment of blinding stupidity, he traded his entire inheritance for a single meal of lentil soup and bread.[3] God later condemned Esau for this foolish decision, labeling him a profane person.[4] In the second story Esau lost his blessing as well. Isaac turned the family business over to Jacob and demoted Esau to the position of being just one of Jacob's employees.[5] Esau was furious, but Jacob was God's obvious choice.

Later in Genesis we find another example of the birthright and the blessing. In chapter 48 Jacob has a private meeting with Joseph and points out that by treating Joseph's two sons as his own, Jacob has effectively given Joseph twice as much as any of his brothers.[6]

A Long Term Goal

Then in Genesis 49 we find Jacob on his deathbed. He calls his sons together to explain to them what will happen after he is gone. Reading this chapter is like sitting in on a board meeting with a wealthy CEO who is about to retire. With no hesitation Jacob names each of his sons and points out their strengths and their weaknesses. He spends extra time talking about Joseph, and then names him as the next patriarch of the family.[7]

Joseph had proven himself able to lead men and able to handle money wisely. Joseph had a good reputation with the government and with the people. Joseph had the spirit of God in his life[8], and God was obviously blessing him. Regardless of his place in the order of birth, Jacob chose Joseph to take over the family business.

Many of the stories of the kings in the Bible are a repeat of the above. David began as a young shepherd and finished as a multimillionaire. Solomon was not David's first-born son, but he was chosen to succeed because of his heart. David gave Solomon an inheritance, and David also gave his son the wisdom to oversee it. Solomon grew the family business by many multiples.

If you think about it, all modern day monarchs are simply carrying on the family business. They are all wealthy – in some cases unbelievably wealthy – and their oldest son or daughter becomes the next king or queen upon their death.

As late as the sixteenth century in Europe, it was common practice for the lord of a manor to choose his heir on his deathbed. The most dependable, business-minded son (or son-in-law) became the new lord of the manor. The other sons often worked for their brother or went into the priesthood, giving their life to the church.

In modern times such situations are extremely rare. We have been duped into believing that our sole concern is having enough retirement funds to make it through the end of our lives. Many Christians die with nothing to leave their children, and occasionally even leave them with an estate bound by debt.

Our present government has graciously relieved us of the responsibility of making our own decisions and financial investments. We make payments into Social Security throughout our entire working lives. We then make withdrawals for the rest of our days. Finally we pass on, leaving little or nothing for our descendants. We have been played the fool.

The vast majority of people are required by law to pay into Social Security. You must obey that law. Some Christians have claimed to have Biblical reasons for flouting the law and for not paying taxes or Social Security. The end result of this course of action is a large fine or a long time in jail. This course of action is not fitting for a child of God. I would like to suggest a careful reading of Romans 13:1-7.

Paying these taxes, however, is not the same as leaving an inheritance. If someone pays into Social Security for 40 or more years and then dies, the day after they die most or all of that money disappears into the huge black hole of government spending. Their descendants receive little or none of it.

It is imperative that everyone have some sort of a savings and investment plan outside of Social Security. A "good man" will take personal responsibility to assure that his children and grandchildren will receive some kind of inheritance.

"House and riches are the inheritance of fathers: and a prudent wife is from the LORD. "   Proverbs 19:14

Pay your taxes and your social security while also investing wisely throughout your working life. Then you can leave an inheritance to your children's children while treating any government benefits you may receive as a bonus.

[1] Genesis 25:5
[2] Genesis 26:12-14
[3] Genesis 25:29-34
[4] Hebrews 12:16

[5] Genesis 27:27-29
[6] Genesis 48:22
[7] Genesis 49:26
[8] Genesis 41:38

Money that Works

In Chapters 1 through 6 you were given some principles to help you to think the right way about money. Then in Chapters 7 through 15 you were shown some principles concerning the handling of your money. If you have implemented those principles, you will now be:

1. Examining the state of your finances every six months.

2. Living by a budget based on percentages and priorities.

3. Paying your tithe first.

4. Eliminating all of your debt.

5. Regularly putting money into a savings account.

6. Finding opportunities to use your money to help others.

7. Enjoying life.

You do not need to rush into investing. Let your savings build up until you have the equivalent of six month's net income in your savings account. This money will be your personal insurance policy for the rest of your life.

Once you have this safety cushion in place, many of the emergencies and problems that plague other people will no longer be a major concern for you. The money will be there to care for any issues that arise. This is your defense against the unexpected.[1] Any money that is withdrawn from this account should be replaced before you begin investing again.

Once this cushion of six month's income is in place, you can begin using any additional savings to earn more money. In other words, you will then begin the transition from working to make money to making money work for you.

In Chapter 13 you were introduced to two different styles of investing: The first style of investing is using your money to buy something that can later be sold for more money. This is called **active investing**. The second style of investing is using your money to buy an investment that will produce a steady stream of income. This is called **passive investing**.

I have a family member who regularly purchases cars that have mechanical problems. He buys the necessary parts, repairs the engines, and sometimes fixes dents or paints the car. He then resells the car for more than he paid for it. Because of his mechanical skills, he has used this style of active investing to make many thousands of dollars.

I have another friend who invests by using online auctions. Using his knowledge of computers and cell phones, he purchases items that he believes to be underpriced and then resells them for a higher price. This is another type of active investing. There are so many ways of active investing that to try to name them all would take another book.

You could purchase materials and then build or make something you can sell. You could write, paint, or draw something you can sell. You could buy and repair something you can sell, or you could buy something and sell it for more by just advertising it better. Most active investing involves adding value before making a profit.

The defining feature of active investing is that you are the one that does it. An electrician may invest his whole life into a small business that earns him many thousands of dollars, but when he retires his income immediately stops. Getting his education and his skill allows him to make money only as long as he is working.

These are all viable methods of **active investing**. These are all possible as long as your knowledge and skill is there to do it. This is active investing because you are actively involved with it. The Bible term for this style of investing is **trading**.[2]

In Matthew 25 Jesus described a master who delivered goods to his three servants and then left, expecting them to care for his goods. The first two men in this parable traded with their master's goods and doubled what they had. These men were active investors.

Active investing can be an excellent way to increase your savings. The disadvantage of active investing is that after every deal is finished, a new deal must be found. My friend may buy a car, repair it, and sell it for thousands of dollars more than he paid for it, but as soon as he is finished he has to find another car to buy and repair.

Although active investing is a good way to make money, you still have to work for your money. The income derived from active investing is a result of you working for your money, and not a result of your money working for you.

The second style of investing is passive investing. Passive investing is using your money to make money with little to no personal involvement. You can do little or nothing and the income from these investments will keep coming.

I have a friend that invests in dividend stocks. Every three months these stocks pay a set amount of money per each share that he owns. This money comes in whether he pays attention to them or not. If he is on vacation, asleep, or even dead, the dividends will continue to be paid.

My friend certainly keeps a close eye on the companies in which he invests, but he may go months without doing anything except counting how much money came in that month. This is an excellent example of having your money work for you.

At one time I was invested in a number of real estate properties. The tenant living in each property paid the rent directly into my business account. The mortgage payment, taxes, and insurance for each property came out of that same account. The money that was left over at the end of each month was my money.

I used my own money to make the down payment on each property, and then borrowed the rest from a bank at a low interest rate. I never tried to fix anything myself. If one of my tenants had a problem with the property, I immediately called a tradesman and had the problem corrected.

These properties took less than three hours of my time each month. This is an example of passive investing. I was not working for that money. Instead, that money was working for me.

In the early stages of your life, you will most likely work for all of your money. You may do this by working a job and receiving a paycheck, or by actively investing. As you get older, your goal should be to convert more and more of your money into passive investments so that your money is working for you.

In Matthew 25:25 the master condemned the third servant because he was wicked and lazy. The servant gave many excuses why he should not be expected to actively invest his lord's money, but there was no reason why he could not have invested it passively. At the very least, he could have put the money in the bank and received interest for it.

You may not have the time or knowledge to actively invest, but with a little study and a little effort you can find some suitable passive investments so that your money can begin working for you. There is no good reason not to do this.

None of the examples in this chapter are suggestions. Just as your opportunities are your own, so your abilities are your own. You have your own level of tolerance for risk. You don't need to try to be a super investor. Just find what works for you.

For many people, this whole idea of passive investing is going to take a major change in thinking. The majority of people with whom I counsel have only one kind of money – *spending money*. Every dollar that they get is going to be spent.

Even when these people save their money, they still think of it as spending money. They are only saving it so that they can spend it later. They are saving for college, or saving for a new car, or saving for a vacation. Even though this money is being saved, it is never going to be transformed into **working money**.

Working money is not being saved to be spent. It is being saved so that it can work for you. It will continue working to earn more money for the rest of your life and beyond. Hopefully, it will still be working when it is handed over to your children and grandchildren.

When someone buys a new car, they hand over a large sum of money and know they will never see that money again. They understand that they have exchanged it for something else. When you transform spending money into working money, you must have the same mentality. That money is gone. It now has a different form and function. Even though it is still measured in dollars, it has been made into thousands of little servants working on your behalf.

Some years ago someone gave my family three chickens. For a long time those chickens laid three eggs a day and when we had saved up enough for a meal we ate the eggs. Then someone loaned us an incubator.

For a couple of weeks we did not eat any eggs. We saved them until we had twenty-six eggs and then we put them all into the incubator. Three weeks later most of those eggs hatched. One egg did not hatch and another one of the chicks died the first day, but the other twenty-four eggs each produced a healthy little chick. About half of the chicks were roosters and so they never produced a single egg.

The rest of the chicks grew up to be hens. After about six months they began laying their own eggs. Now instead of getting two or three eggs each morning, we were getting twelve to fifteen eggs. The point of this story is that you cannot eat an egg and hatch it too. You have to decide what you are going to do with that egg. Saving and hatching it will eventually produce a lot more eggs.

In the same way, you have to decide what you are going to do with each dollar that you make. You can spend it and enjoy the pleasure of whatever it is that you buy, or you can invest it and enjoy getting more dollars from your investment.[3]

Now when I look at an egg, I can see the potential hidden within. If that egg were hatched instead of eaten, it might one day become a chicken which could lay more eggs.

When you hold a dollar in your hand, what do you see? Do you only see the pleasure that can be obtained by spending it, or can you see the potential of what that dollar could one day produce if it were invested wisely?

Just like our chickens, not all of your investments will produce. Some may fail, and you may lose money. You do not have to succeed 100% of the time to be a good investor. You do need to be patient and keep working at it. One day you may find that your **working money** is making more money than you are.

[1]Ecclesiastes 7:12
[2]Matthew 25:16
[3]Ecclesiastes 11:1, 2

THE NEXT GENERATION

As God's steward you are responsible for handling His money in a way that is pleasing to Him. If the Lord has blessed you with children, then you are also a steward of your children. You have been given the responsibility to raise them up in the nurture and admonition of the Lord.

"And, ye fathers, provoke not your children to wrath: but bring them up in the nurture and admonition of the Lord." Ephesians 6:4

A parent who is a faithful steward of their money but an unfaithful steward of their children will disappoint their Master. They will build up an inheritance that will eventually be squandered or lost by their children.

A parent who is a faithful steward of their children but an unfaithful steward of their money will likewise disappoint their Master. Their children may love God and have wisdom, but they will never receive an inheritance.

Someone who is an unfaithful steward of both their money and their children will doubly disappoint their Master. They will have lost an opportunity to make an impact for the Lord on following generations.

My desire is that you are a faithful steward with both your money and your children. Like Abraham, Isaac, Jacob, and David, you will be able to hand over an inheritance to your children who have been well trained to deal with it.

BEGIN WITH AN ALLOWANCE

As each of my children reached their ninth birthday, two very special things happened. First, they received an allowance for the first time. Second, they got a short lesson from their father to teach them what they were supposed to do with it.

As I gave each of my children their first allowance, I explained to them that they were now old enough to be a working part of the family. Not only would they continue to do their regular duties around the house, but they would now be paid for it. Ninth birthdays have always been a very special day in our household.

You and I both know that you are already providing your child with room and board, transportation, clothing, an education, and a hundred other things, but paying your child for the work they do around the house is not the main reason for giving them an allowance.

The main reason for giving your child an allowance is to provide you with the opportunity to teach them how to use a budget, how to tithe, how to save, and how to invest. The best way to teach your child about money is to put some of it in their little hands.

USE GIFTS AS TEACHING TIMES

When your children receive money as gifts for Christmas or on their birthdays, sit down with them and teach them how to calculate their tithe and savings. At this point in their lives they will not have any debt, so they should tithe 10% and put 20% into savings. Doing this every time they receive any money will engrave it into their minds and make it a part of their lives.

"Train up a child in the way he should go: and when he is old, he will not depart from it."   Proverbs 22:6

Explain to them why they are tithing. Teach them how it proves to God that they trust Him. If your church prints a monthly budget, you can use that to show your child where their tithe goes and how it is used to do God's work.

Buy them a bank where they can keep their savings. Take their money out occasionally and count it with them so they can see how it grows. Remind them how this money will help them in the future.

Remember to show them that they still get to keep 70% to do with as they like. This is their money. This is also a great time to teach them to begin giving to others.

HELP YOUR CHILDREN TO EARN MONEY

Providing a way for your children to earn money will often be more work for you than it is for them. Helping your son to take your lawnmower somewhere so that he can earn money cutting the grass may seem like a bother now, but you will be teaching him to have a good work ethic. You will also be helping him to learn the value of money.

When your teenage daughter wants to babysit to earn an income, it may involve you transporting her both ways. It will be worth the effort when she is able to take care of herself and her own finances later in life.

I am eternally grateful for the sacrifice that my parents made to make sure that I could have my first paper route when I was only twelve. I am sure that it was often more of a hindrance than a help to them. Many of the principles that my father taught me were first applied to those few dollars that I made delivering those papers.

When my oldest son was still young, we bought four calves. He paid for one of the calves, and I paid for its hay and feed. When the calf was fully grown, he sold it and paid my portion back. He invested his profits and later used them to help pay the tuition for his first year at college. The small effort that I made repaid itself many times over.

READ THIS BOOK TO YOUR CHILDREN

Most of these lessons are simple enough for a child to understand. Reading a chapter together each evening will allow you to finish the whole book in less than three weeks. Discussing what you read will show your children that you care about their future.

TALK WITH YOUR CHILDREN ABOUT MONEY

Show your children your paycheck. Explain how your taxes get taken out and sent to the government before you get paid. Teach them about Social Security and explain what it can and cannot do. Explain the difference between a credit card and a debit card. Take them to an ATM and show them how to take money out. Teach them how to write a check.

Before you make your next investment, sit down and explain it to your children. If you are not able to make them understand it in less than ten minutes, it is probably too complicated anyway. Have them sit down with you one afternoon while you pay your bills for the month. Your children will probably learn about most of these things eventually, but it is so much better for them to learn from their own parents.

You may be pleasantly surprised to see a change in your children's attitude. Your children will respect you when they see that you are in control of your personal finances and that you are able to teach them how to handle theirs. Their attitude towards you may also improve when they begin to understand that they could one day receive a significant sum of money from you.

PREPARE YOUR CHILDREN FOR THEIR FUTURE

If you follow the lessons in this book and teach your children to do the same, your grandchildren's financial situation may one day be very different from yours. Can you imagine a generation of Christian young people that have a desire to do something great for God and the financial independence to do it? You may be hindered from using all of your time to serve God because you are forced to work for a living, but you may be able to give your descendants the freedom to do so.

"Wisdom is good with an inheritance: and by it there is profit to them that see the sun." Ecclesiastes 7:11

Defining Success

The preceding chapters have been written so that you can use these principles for your whole life, and the results are intended to live on long after you are gone. They are presented in this format in order that they might be immediately usable no matter what your financial situation is today.

As you begin to implement the principles contained in this book, do not lose sight of your ultimate goal. Your ultimate goal is that you are a good steward, that God is pleased with how you take care of what He has entrusted to you, and that He will one day say, "Well done, thou good and faithful servant."

If you are carrying a heavy load of debt, you may be tempted to change the methods taught here in order to get yourself out of debt as quickly as possible. Although living debt free should be one of your goals, it is more important that you handle your finances correctly THIS month.

If you are opening a new savings account, you may be tempted to change the methods taught here in order to grow the balance of that account as quickly as possible. Although having a savings account with six month's income in it is one of your goals, it is more important that you handle your finances correctly THIS month.

If you are considering investing, your mind may be swimming with ideas how you can begin trading, or how you can begin making your money earn money for you and start bringing in a passive income. Although creating a steady stream of passive income is one of your goals, it is more important that you handle your finances correctly THIS month.

Do not let yourself be seduced by the desire to reach a particular number or a particular goal or however much that you feel is "enough." Never forget that you are going to leave it all here when you go. You are just taking care of it while you are here.

Do not fall into the trap of comparing your finances with those of other Christians. Remember that the servant who used two talents to gain two more talents received the same commendation as the servant who used five talents to gain five more talents.

Success in God's kingdom is not measured with dollars, but with obedience. Here are some questions that you can ask yourself in order to determine whether you are presently succeeding with your finances.

1. Do you have a fairly good idea of where you are today with your finances?

2. Do you carefully calculate your budget each month or as often as you are paid?

3. Do you faithfully tithe on everything you make?

4. Are you in the process of eliminating all of your debt?

5. Do you have, or are you working towards having, the equivalent of six month's net income in a savings account?

6. Are you able to help other people when you see the opportunity or when the Lord lays a need on your heart?

7. Are you able to spend the remaining 70% of your income without guilt because you handled the first 30% correctly?

8. Are you converting your treasures into cash that can be used to buy the things you really need, given away, or invested?

9. Are you looking for investments that will eventually provide you with a steady stream of passive income?

10. Are you training your children to handle their finances correctly?

The more times that you can answer "yes" to these questions, the closer you are to being a success in the area of your finances.

Thank you for taking the time to read this book. It is my sincere desire that we can one day stand side by side in front of our Master, and that we will both hear the words, "Well done."

159 Verses from Proverbs

1:13, 14 (2 verses) *We shall find all precious substance, we shall fill our houses with spoil: Cast in thy lot among us; let us all have one purse:*

1:19 (1 verse) *So are the ways of every one that is greedy of gain; which taketh away the life of the owners thereof.*

1:32 (1 verse) *For the turning away of the simple shall slay them, and the prosperity of fools shall destroy them.*

2:4 (1 verse) *If thou seekest her as silver, and searchest for her as for hid treasures;*

3:9, 10 (2 verses) *Honour the LORD with thy substance, and with the firstfruits of all thine increase: So shall thy barns be filled with plenty, and thy presses shall burst out with new wine.*

3:14-16 (3 verses) *For the merchandise of it is better than the merchandise of silver, and the gain thereof than fine gold. She is more precious than rubies: and all the things thou canst desire are not to be compared unto her. Length of days is in her right hand; and in her left hand riches and honour.*

5:10 (1 verse) *Lest strangers be filled with thy wealth; and thy labours be in the house of a stranger;*

6:1-5 (5 verses) *My son, if thou be surety for thy friend, if thou hast stricken thy hand with a stranger, Thou art snared with the words of thy mouth, thou art taken with the words of thy mouth. Do this now, my son, and deliver thyself, when thou art come into the hand of thy friend; go, humble thyself, and make sure thy friend. Give not sleep to thine eyes, nor slumber to thine eyelids. Deliver thyself as a roe from the hand of the hunter, and as a bird from the hand of the fowler.*

6:6-11 (6 verses) *Go to the ant, thou sluggard; consider her ways, and be wise: Which having no guide, overseer, or ruler, Provideth her meat in the summer, and gathereth her food in the harvest. How long wilt thou sleep, O sluggard? when wilt thou arise out of thy sleep? Yet a little sleep, a little slumber, a little folding of the hands to sleep: So shall thy poverty come as one that travelleth, and thy want as an armed man.*

6:30, 31 (2 verses) *Men do not despise a thief, if he steal to satisfy his soul when he is hungry; But if he be found, he shall restore sevenfold; he shall give all the substance of his house.*

6:35 (1 verse) *He will not regard any ransom; neither will he rest content, though thou givest many gifts.*

7:14 (1 verse) *I have peace offerings with me; this day have I payed my vows.*

7:20 (1 verse) *He hath taken a bag of money with him, and will come home at the day appointed.*

8:10, 11 (2 verses) *Receive my instruction, and not silver; and knowledge rather than choice gold. For wisdom is better than rubies; and all the things that may be desired are not to be compared to it.*

8:18, 19 (2 verses) *Riches and honour are with me; yea, durable riches and righteousness. My fruit is better than gold, yea, than fine gold; and my revenue than choice silver.*

8:21 (1 verse) *That I may cause those that love me to inherit substance; and I will fill their treasures.*

10:2-4 (3 verses) *Treasures of wickedness profit nothing: but righteousness delivereth from death. The LORD will not suffer the soul of the righteous to famish: but he casteth away the substance of the wicked. He becometh poor that dealeth with a slack hand: but the hand of the diligent maketh rich.*

10:15 (1 verse) *The rich man's wealth is his strong city: the destruction of the poor is their poverty.*

10:20 (1 verse) *The tongue of the just is as choice silver: the heart of the wicked is little worth.*

10:22 (1 verse) *The blessing of the LORD, it maketh rich, and he addeth no sorrow with it.*

11:4 (1 verse) *Riches profit not in the day of wrath: but righteousness delivereth from death.*

11:15, 16 (2 verses) *He that is surety for a stranger shall smart for it: and he that hateth suretiship is sure. A gracious woman retaineth honour: and strong men retain riches.*

11:24-26 (3 verses) *There is that scattereth, and yet increaseth; and there is that withholdeth more than is meet, but it tendeth to poverty. The liberal soul shall be made fat: and he that watereth shall be watered also himself. He that withholdeth corn, the people shall curse him: but blessing shall be upon the head of him that selleth it.*

11:28 (1 verse) *He that trusteth in his riches shall fall: but the righteous shall flourish as a branch.*

12:24 (1 verse) *The hand of the diligent shall bear rule: but the slothful shall be under tribute.*

12:27 (1 verse) *The slothful man roasteth not that which he took in hunting: but the substance of a diligent man is precious.*

13:7, 8 (2 verses) *There is that maketh himself rich, yet hath nothing: there is that maketh himself poor, yet hath great riches. The ransom of a man's life are his riches: but the poor heareth not rebuke.*

13:11 (1 verse) *Wealth gotten by vanity shall be diminished: but he that gathereth by labour shall increase.*

13:18 (1 verse) *Poverty and shame shall be to him that refuseth instruction: but he that regardeth reproof shall be honoured.*

13:22, 23 (2 verses) *A good man leaveth an inheritance to his children's children: and the wealth of the sinner is laid up for the just. Much food is in the tillage of the poor: but there is that is destroyed for want of judgment.*

14:20, 21 (2 verses) *The poor is hated even of his own neighbour: but the rich hath many friends. He that despiseth his neighbour sinneth: but he that hath mercy on the poor, happy is he.*

14:23, 24 (2 verses) *In all labour there is profit: but the talk of the lips tendeth only to penury. The crown of the wise is their riches: but the foolishness of fools is folly.*

14:31 (1 verse) *He that oppresseth the poor reproacheth his Maker: but he that honoureth him hath mercy on the poor.*

15:6 (1 verse) *In the house of the righteous is much treasure: but in the revenues of the wicked is trouble.*

15:16 (1 verse) *Better is little with the fear of the LORD than great treasure and trouble therewith.*

15:27 (1 verse) *He that is greedy of gain troubleth his own house; but he that hateth gifts shall live.*

16:8 (1 verse) *Better is a little with righteousness than great revenues without right.*

16:11 (1 verse) *A just weight and balance are the LORD'S: all the weights of the bag are his work.*

16:16 (1 verse) *How much better is it to get wisdom than gold! and to get understanding rather to be chosen than silver!*

16:19 (1 verse) *Better it is to be of an humble spirit with the lowly, than to divide the spoil with the proud.*

17:2, 3 (2 verses) *A wise servant shall have rule over a son that causeth shame, and shall have part of the inheritance among the brethren. The fining pot is for silver, and the furnace for gold: but the LORD trieth the hearts.*

17:5 (1 verse) *Whoso mocketh the poor reproacheth his Maker: and he that is glad at calamities shall not be unpunished.*

17:8 (1 verse) *A gift is as a precious stone in the eyes of him that hath it: whithersoever it turneth, it prospereth.*

17:16 (1 verse) *Wherefore is there a price in the hand of a fool to get wisdom, seeing he hath no heart to it?*

17:18 (1 verse) *A man void of understanding striketh hands, and becometh surety in the presence of his friend.*

17:23 (1 verse) *A wicked man taketh a gift out of the bosom to pervert the ways of judgment.*

18:11 (1 verse) *The rich man's wealth is his strong city, and as an high wall in his own conceit.*

18:23 (1 verse) *The poor useth intreaties; but the rich answereth roughly.*

19:1 (1 verse) *Better is the poor that walketh in his integrity, than he that is perverse in his lips, and is a fool.*

19:4 (1 verse) *Wealth maketh many friends; but the poor is separated from his neighbour.*

19:7 (1 verse) *All the brethren of the poor do hate him: how much more do his friends go far from him? he pursueth them with words, yet they are wanting to him.*

19:14 (1 verse) *House and riches are the inheritance of fathers: and a prudent wife is from the LORD.*

19:17 (1 verse) *He that hath pity upon the poor lendeth unto the LORD; and that which he hath given will he pay him again.*

19:22 (1 verse) *The desire of a man is his kindness: and a poor man is better than a liar.*

20:13-16 (4 verses) *Love not sleep, lest thou come to poverty; open thine eyes, and thou shalt be satisfied with bread. It is naught, it is naught, saith the buyer: but when he is gone his way, then he boasteth. There is gold, and a multitude of rubies: but the lips of knowledge are a precious jewel. Take his garment that is surety for a stranger: and take a pledge of him for a strange woman.*

20:21 (1 verse) *An inheritance may be gotten hastily at the beginning; but the end thereof shall not be blessed.*

21:5-7 (3 verses) *The thoughts of the diligent tend only to plenteousness; but of every one that is hasty only to want. The getting of treasures by a lying tongue is a vanity tossed to and fro of them that seek death. The robbery of the wicked shall destroy them; because they refuse to do judgment.*

21:13, 14 (2 verses) Whoso stoppeth his ears at the cry of the poor, he also shall cry himself, but shall not be heard. A gift in secret pacifieth anger: and a reward in the bosom strong wrath.

21:17 (1 verse) He that loveth pleasure shall be a poor man: he that loveth wine and oil shall not be rich.

21:20 (1 verse) There is treasure to be desired and oil in the dwelling of the wise; but a foolish man spendeth it up.

22:1-4 (4 verses) A good name is rather to be chosen than great riches, and loving favour rather than silver and gold. The rich and poor meet together: the LORD is the maker of them all. A prudent man foreseeth the evil, and hideth himself: but the simple pass on, and are punished. By humility and the fear of the LORD are riches, and honour, and life.

22:7 (1 verse) The rich ruleth over the poor, and the borrower is servant to the lender.

22:9 (1 verse) He that hath a bountiful eye shall be blessed; for he giveth of his bread to the poor.

22:16 (1 verse) He that oppresseth the poor to increase his riches, and he that giveth to the rich, shall surely come to want.

22:22, 23 (2 verses) Rob not the poor, because he is poor: neither oppress the afflicted in the gate: For the LORD will plead their cause, and spoil the soul of those that spoiled them.

22:26, 27 (2 verses) Be not thou one of them that strike hands, or of them that are sureties for debts. If thou hast nothing to pay, why should he take away thy bed from under thee?

22:29 (1 verse) Seest thou a man diligent in his business? he shall stand before kings; he shall not stand before mean men.

23:4, 5 (2 verses) *Labour not to be rich: cease from thine own wisdom. Wilt thou set thine eyes upon that which is not? for riches certainly make themselves wings; they fly away as an eagle toward heaven.*

23:21 (1 verse) *For the drunkard and the glutton shall come to poverty: and drowsiness shall clothe a man with rags.*

23:23 (1 verse) *Buy the truth, and sell it not; also wisdom, and instruction, and understanding.*

24:3, 4 (2 verses) *Through wisdom is an house builded; and by understanding it is established: And by knowledge shall the chambers be filled with all precious and pleasant riches.*

24:27 (1 verse) *Prepare thy work without, and make it fit for thyself in the field; and afterwards build thine house.*

24:30-34 (5 verses) *I went by the field of the slothful, and by the vineyard of the man void of understanding; And, lo, it was all grown over with thorns, and nettles had covered the face thereof, and the stone wall thereof was broken down. Then I saw, and considered it well: I looked upon it, and received instruction. Yet a little sleep, a little slumber, a little folding of the hands to sleep: So shall thy poverty come as one that travelleth; and thy want as an armed man.*

27:13 (1 verse) *Take his garment that is surety for a stranger, and take a pledge of him for a strange woman.*

27:23-27 (5 verses) *Be thou diligent to know the state of thy flocks, and look well to thy herds. For riches are not for ever: and doth the crown endure to every generation? The hay appeareth, and the tender grass sheweth itself, and herbs of the mountains are gathered. The lambs are for thy clothing, and the goats are the price of the field. And thou shalt have goats' milk enough for thy food, for the food of thy household, and for the maintenance for thy maidens.*

28:3 (1 verse) *A poor man that oppresseth the poor is like a sweeping rain which leaveth no food.*

28:6 (1 verse) *Better is the poor that walketh in his uprightness, than he that is perverse in his ways, though he be rich.*

28:8 (1 verse) *He that by usury and unjust gain increaseth his substance, he shall gather it for him that will pity the poor.*

28:11 (1 verse) *The rich man is wise in his own conceit; but the poor that hath understanding searcheth him out.*

28:15, 16 (2 verses) *As a roaring lion, and a ranging bear; so is a wicked ruler over the poor people. The prince that wanteth understanding is also a great oppressor: but he that hateth covetousness shall prolong his days.*

28:19-20 (2 verses) *He that tilleth his land shall have plenty of bread: but he that followeth after vain persons shall have poverty enough. A faithful man shall abound with blessings: but he that maketh haste to be rich shall not be innocent.*

28:22 (1 verse) *He that hasteth to be rich hath an evil eye, and considereth not that poverty shall come upon him.*

28:24 (1 verse) *Whoso robbeth his father or his mother, and saith, It is no transgression; the same is the companion of a destroyer.*

28:27 (1 verse) *He that giveth unto the poor shall not lack: but he that hideth his eyes shall have many a curse.*

29:3, 4 (2 verses) *Whoso loveth wisdom rejoiceth his father: but he that keepeth company with harlots spendeth his substance. The king by judgment establisheth the land: but he that receiveth gifts overthroweth it.*

29:7 (1 verse) *The righteous considereth the cause of the poor: but the wicked regardeth not to know it.*

29:13, 14 (2 verses) *The poor and the deceitful man meet together: the LORD lighteneth both their eyes. The king that faithfully judgeth the poor, his throne shall be established for ever.*

29:24 (1 verse) *Whoso is partner with a thief hateth his own soul: he heareth cursing, and bewrayeth it not.*

30:7-9 (3 verses) *Two things have I required of thee; deny me them not before I die: Remove far from me vanity and lies: give me neither poverty nor riches; feed me with food convenient for me: Lest I be full, and deny thee, and say, Who is the LORD? or lest I be poor, and steal, and take the name of my God in vain.*

30:14 (1 verse) *There is a generation, whose teeth are as swords, and their jaw teeth as knives, to devour the poor from off the earth, and the needy from among men.*

31:9 (1 verse) *Open thy mouth, judge righteously, and plead the cause of the poor and needy.*

31:10-24 (15 verses) *Who can find a virtuous woman? for her price is far above rubies. The heart of her husband doth safely trust in her, so that he shall have no need of spoil. She will do him good and not evil all the days of her life. She seeketh wool, and flax, and worketh willingly with her hands. She is like the merchants' ships; she bringeth her food from afar. She riseth also while it is yet night, and giveth meat to her household, and a portion to her maidens. She considereth a field, and buyeth it: with the fruit of her hands she planteth a vineyard. She girdeth her loins with strength, and strengtheneth her arms. She perceiveth that her merchandise is good: her candle goeth not out by night. She layeth her hands to the spindle, and her hands hold the distaff. She stretcheth out her hand to the poor; yea, she reacheth forth her hands to the needy.*

She is not afraid of the snow for her household: for all her household are clothed with scarlet. She maketh herself coverings of tapestry; her clothing is silk and purple. Her husband is known in the gates, when he sitteth among the elders of the land. She maketh fine linen, and selleth it; and delivereth girdles unto the merchant.

Financial Worksheets

Financial Worksheets

Worksheet 1 – Income

Income Source	Weekly	Bi-weekly	Monthly
Salary	_____	_____	_____
Wages	_____	_____	_____
Social Security	_____	_____	_____
Benefits	_____	_____	_____
Pension	_____	_____	_____
Rental income	_____	_____	_____
Royalties	_____	_____	_____
Interest	_____	_____	_____
Dividends	_____	_____	_____
Other	_____	_____	_____
Other	_____	_____	_____
Other	_____	_____	_____
Total	(_____)	(_____)	_____

Multiply Weekly total by 52 and divide by 12   (_____)

Multiply Bi-weekly Total by 26 and divide by 12   (_____)

Grand Total   _____

WORKSHEET 2 – BILLS

Bill	Weekly	Bi-weekly	Monthly
Tithe	_____	_____	_____
Income Taxes	_____	_____	_____
Social Security	_____	_____	_____
State Taxes	_____	_____	_____
Mortgage/Rent	_____	_____	_____
Life Insurance	_____	_____	_____
Utilities	_____	_____	_____
Telephone/Internet	_____	_____	_____
Cable	_____	_____	_____
Prescriptions	_____	_____	_____
Missions/Charities	_____	_____	_____
Other	_____	_____	_____
Total	(_____)	(_____)	_____

Multiply Weekly total by 52 and divide by 12   (_____)

Multiply Bi-weekly Total by 26 and divide by 12   (_____)

Grand Total   _____

Worksheet 3 – Debts

Your debts are those bills that have an end date. Debts include all credit card balances, car payments, personal loans, bank loans, medical bills, student loans, and borrowed money. You should also include any mortgage with less than five years to pay.

Debt Owed	Total Owed	Min. Payment	Interest Rate
_____	_____	_____	_____
_____	_____	_____	_____
_____	_____	_____	_____
_____	_____	_____	_____
_____	_____	_____	_____
_____	_____	_____	_____
_____	_____	_____	_____
_____	_____	_____	_____
_____	_____	_____	_____
_____	_____	_____	_____
_____	_____	_____	_____

Total _____ _____

The Birthright and the Blessing

WORKSHEET 4 – POSSESSIONS

What You Own   **Present Resale Value**

_____   _____

_____   _____

_____   _____

_____   _____

_____   _____

_____   _____

_____   _____

_____   _____

_____   _____

_____   _____

_____   _____

Total amount of money you have $ _____

Total Value

Worksheet 5 – Assets

Income	Monthly	Quarterly	Annual
Savings Account	_____	_____	_____
Rental Properties	_____	_____	_____
Home Businesses	_____	_____	_____
Royalties	_____	_____	_____
Dividends	_____	_____	_____
Bonds	_____	_____	_____
Other	_____	_____	_____
Other	_____	_____	_____
Other	_____	_____	_____
Other	_____	_____	_____
Other	_____	_____	_____
Other	_____	_____	_____
Total	_____	_____	_____

Divide Quarterly Income by 3   (_____)

Divide Annual Income by 12   (_____)

Grand Total   _____

WORKSHEET 6 – CASH FLOW

Determining Your Financial State

1. How often do you get paid? _____

2. What is your total income each month? _____

3. What are your total bills each month? _____

4. What are your total debts? _____

5. What are your total minimum payments? _____

First: Add the totals from 3 and 5 _____

Second: Subtract that total from 2 _____

Total Income – (Total Bills + Total Minimum Payments)

You should recalculate a new Cash Flow statement
at least once every six months.

Worksheet 7 – Balance Sheet

Determining Your Financial State

Total value of possessions on Worksheet 4   _____

Total owed in second column on Worksheet 3   _____

Subtract   _____

Net Worth = Total of what I own – Total of what I owe

You should recalculate a new Balance Sheet statement at least once every six months.

NOTES

Made in the USA
Monee, IL
08 November 2021